Lost
and
Found

23 Things
You Can Do
to Find
Personal Freedom

Dr. Arthur Caliandro
with Barry Lenson

McGraw-Hill

New York   Chicago   San Francisco   Lisbon   London
Madrid   Mexico City   Milan   New Delhi   San Juan
Seoul   Singapore   Sydney   Toronto

1 2 3 4 5 6 7 8 9 0   AGM/AGM   0 9 8 7 6 5 4 3

ISBN 0-07-140862-2

McGraw-Hill books are available at special quantity discounts to use as premiums and sales promotions, or for use in corporate training programs. For more information, please write to the Director of Special Sales, Professional Publishing, McGraw-Hill, Two Penn Plaza, New York, NY 10121-2298. Or contact your local bookstore.

 This book is printed on recycled, acid-free paper containing a minimum of 50% recycled, de-inked fiber.

Library of Congress Cataloging-in-Publication Data

Caliandro, Arthur.
   Lost and found : 23 things you can do to find personal freedom / Arthur Caliandro with Barry Lenson. — 1st ed.
      p. cm.
   ISBN 0-07-140862-2 (hardcover : alk. paper)
   1. Self-actualization (Psychology) I. Lenson, Barry. II. Title.
   BF637.S4.C32 2003
   158—dc22

                                                    2003018132

To the congregation
of the Marble Collegiate Church,
an extraordinarily dynamic spiritual community
that has loved, nurtured, and taught me so much
about life, love, faith, and peace

Contents

Acknowledgments

I send heartfelt thanks to all the people who lent their good wishes, encouragement, and support for this book. There are also some special champions of this project to whom I want to express my special thanks.

Susan Eldred and Kathleen Taylor, invaluable members of my staff at Marble Collegiate Church, for their steady help and support at every stage.

Nancy Hancock at McGraw-Hill, for lending ideas and enthusiasm to make this a far better book.

Meg Leder and Jane Palmieri of McGraw-Hill, for reliably helping me navigate every stage of the publishing and production processes.

Gareth Esersky, my wise agent, for tending to all the business details so I could focus on the hard work of writing.

Martha Doty, executive director of MarbleVision, for helping to make sure that this book and its message reach as many people as possible.

The many people whose stories are an integral part of this book. I cannot name you all, but you have truly given life to this book.

Most of all, I thank my wonderful wife Lea for her encouragement and patience during my months of work and writing. Without your support and love, this book would not exist.

Dr. Arthur Caliandro

Introduction

We Americans love our freedom. We love living in a country where we can speak what is on our minds. We value our right to choose our leaders. We cherish our religious freedom.

We are privileged to live in this land, where both privacy and individual rights are protected. Even when these rights are being challenged, there is always recourse in our democratic system.

Freedom is treasured here. It is precious. That is why we are willing to make such sacrifices when we see it threatened.

Yet we are still struggling with one puzzling thing about freedom: All the remarkable freedoms we enjoy in America do not always make us free personally. It is possible to be hampered, tied up, unhappy, and limited in America, despite all the freedoms we enjoy.

Where does personal freedom come from? It does not come from without, but from within. It comes from choices we make, and often it involves considerable self-discipline.

As a minister I do a great deal of public speaking, and I always speak without a manuscript or notes. Often, people say that my words seem to come easily and naturally. A man once told me that I always seem to be so free when I speak. If they only knew about all the effort that makes that impression of ease possible! The times that I feel the greatest freedom when speaking, when I feel most in control of myself and my material, are those times when I was best prepared. That preparation demands an enormous number of hours spent thinking, reading, and processing, not to mention the time I spend doubting myself, my material, and the words I will use to express my message.

Still I like the incredible freedom I feel after I have done all that hard preparation. Do I also like the sweat, anxiety, self-doubt, and the hours I had to invest in order to feel so free? No, not always. I sometimes resent giving up things I love to do. I can't watch Saturday afternoon football games. I can't go out to dinner or have a social evening with friends on a Saturday night because that sermon I will give the next morning has consumed me so completely.

Yet those are small sacrifices I have learned to put in perspective. My freedom and any effectiveness I have as a preacher, or any lack thereof, are the direct result of how much disciplined work and preparation I am willing to invest.

Freedom can only come after such long, hard work. But I am willing to say loud and clear: the results are always worth it. Such is the nature of personal freedom.

This book is about that journey to freedom. As I said at the outset, we don't just receive freedom. It is never simply given to us. We have to engage in what can sometimes be exhaustive personal work to earn it.

Before we begin, let me say that your journey to personal freedom can never be the same as mine, because we are different people. We each have different strengths, weaknesses, and areas we need to discover and explore—our individual "freedom blocks," if you will. Freedom follows when they are discovered and rolled out of the way.

My hope and prayer is that through work and exploration we will all come to enjoy personal freedom. It is a process I am working on, and you can work on it too. Through this book, it is my hope that we deepen our commitment to that journey together.

1

Freedom Follows Banishing Worry

---

*W*orry is an insidious demon, a formidable foe. It is artful and wily, and if you give it free rein over your life, it will disable you and lead to despair. It takes hard work to banish worry from your life, but when you do, you empower yourself to cope with life's difficulties and challenges in a higher, more effective and joyous way.

In my mind's eye, I am envisioning a man I know very well. Let me describe him to you. His brow is rutted with permanent furrows. The muscles of his face and neck are so taut, they resemble rocks. His gait is slow and measured. His head is always down, and he seems uptight and preoccupied. When I describe him, he sounds almost unreal, somewhat like a caricature. But I really do know him, and when I describe him, I am not exaggerating.

What is wrong with him? Does he have a back problem? A debilitating disease? No, his problem is something else entirely.

He has given his life over to worry. You might even say he has become a leading expert on the subject. What does he worry about? Everything! He worries about his family. He worries about his spouse—her health and her attitude. He worries about his own health, even though his worrying has caused the greatest share of his ills. He worries about bad weather, which always seems to strike when he is planning to drive somewhere. He worries about his boss, whom he says he cannot trust. He worries about the holidays and how unhappy they might turn out to be. He worries about winter. He worries about dinner. He worries

about money. He worries about his son's marriage and his choice
of a wife.

I could go on forever listing all the things that this man worries about, but I will stop here because you are surely getting the
idea. He worries about *everything*. Worry, in fact, has become the
"filter" he places between himself and all life activities. Nothing
passes into his consciousness unless it first passes through that
worry filter, which sorts out all the good parts and allows only the
bad to get through. Nothing passes out from him, in terms of
action in the world, unless it has been diminished and shaped and
colored by that same worry filter. He is so mired in worry, it
would be difficult to imagine what he might be like if it suddenly went away.

Yes, worry is an insidious enemy. It often begins with the best
of intentions. After all, healthy worry (perhaps "concern" would
be a better word for it) can be a way of expressing commitment
to people we love or of making sure our money and other essential resources are safe and well cared for. But unless we maintain
perspective on our tendencies to worry and keep them healthy
and positive, worry often seizes control. The results can be truly
devastating.

Let's pause for a moment and do a quick worry "inventory"
of all the harm we do ourselves when we worry compulsively:

- *We lose sight of what is best in our lives.* Instead of seeing
  all the good things that surround us, we become fixated
  on the bad. We get mired in negativism. The world
  becomes a dark, threatening, and hopeless place.

- *We harm our friendships and loving relationships.* I cannot
  abide being around a chronic worrier for long, and I
  imagine that you cannot either. Worry drives people away.

- *We do serious damage to the people who love us the most.*
  When we do not drive people away by worrying, we still
  manage to harm them. The lives of our friends and loved
  ones become infected by our own worry phobias.

Worriers are people who won't take their kids to the ball game (too worried to drive that far!), refinance their homes (might get turned down!), start a new business (it will never work!), or get homes repaired (home fix-up people are dishonest!). For worriers, it is safer to stay stuck and drag down all the people around them.

- *We limit our success because we cannot move forward with our careers and other plans.* Worriers cannot take risks, and as a result, they usually stay stuck in disadvantageous situations. Worry and failure might well be one and the same thing.

- *We harm our own health through stress.* Much has been written about the great harm that is done to us by chronic stress and worry—heart disease, ulcers, strokes, and other serious outcomes. An old friend of mine who lived to an advanced age once told me what her secret was: "I have learned not to worry!" What health and wisdom reside in those words.

- *We feel worthless in the eyes of the world.* Because people who are stalled by worry never act, their inertia finally leads them to lowered self-esteem. "I worry about doing that" quickly turns to "I cannot do that" as any sense of self-efficacy disappears.

- *We lose a sense of the bigger picture of what matters most in our lives.* Worriers cannot focus on the things that really matter a lot to most people, even such fundamental assets as family, career, helping others, admiring art, or pursuing hobbies. Low-level worries, like a low-lying black cloud, block the view of all that might make life really worthwhile.

How then can we chase away this demon and keep it from causing such damage in our lives? Over the years, I have asked successful, nonworrying people how they handle worry, and I have gotten some remarkable answers.

People who have beaten worry tell me that the first vital step is to admit that you are worrying. Admit that you are a worrier! Drop any defensive denials, and confront the fact that you really are worrying. Refuse to look the other way or avoid the topic.

We know that in the successful 12-step programs, the first step toward overcoming a problem is to admit it, to say, "I have this problem I cannot control, it is bigger than I am." Similarly, saying openly, "Worry has gotten a hold on me" is the first step toward chasing it away. Yet I'm surprised that the topic of worry is off-limits for so many people. I'll talk to people who are otherwise growing and stretching in various areas in their lives, but when the conversation turns to worry, they seem to say, "You don't get to touch me and my worrying. That is off-limits!" Worry has become off-limits for them and given a protected status. I don't understand why these people are so devoted to worry. Perhaps they derive pleasure from feeling badly.

If you want to get rid of worry, you've got to take it out of the back pocket, take it out of the cellar, take it out of the freezer so that you can free yourself to process it and get beyond it.

The next vital step is to take action. Because worry and action cannot exist side by side.

Some years ago, I was talking with an actor about his career. As you know, there is practically no security in being an actor. Even the most successful among them have no guarantees that they will continue to work for long.

It would seem logical that actors would worry all the time, wouldn't it, in light of all those uncertainties. Yet the actor friend I spoke with explained to me that it was not so for him. And he explained to me his personal recipe for keeping worry from immobilizing him and his career.

He told me that when he was a young actor, he came to New York to find work. He was fresh from successes in summer stock. He had his good reviews. He was on a wonderful roll, and he was ready to take on the world!

But when he got to the city, things didn't work out too well. He went to audition after audition. Some went very well, others less so. He sat around expecting his phone to start ringing off the hook. But the calls never came. He began to worry. Then a friend advised him, "You've got to get busy."

"Busy at what? What am I supposed to do?" he asked.

"Busy at what you're all about as a person! Go to classes, write a play, talk to people, share ideas. Don't just sit there waiting for someone to call. Get out there and get busy, and things will start to happen!"

So he did just that. He took classes, met people, and talked about acting and theater all day long. Soon he noticed that all his new activity had quieted his worries. Then he began to notice that everything he was doing was bringing him into contact with new opportunities and new people. In time, things really began to happen for him. Now, he is usually very busy and in demand. In those times when things get slow, he makes himself even busier and more active. This has been the secret of a rewarding career that has lasted for decades. And you may notice that worry played no part in his success.

So take action. Get busy. You will be surprised to see that often, the rest will take care of itself and worry will quietly exit— a character that has no longer has a role to play in your life.

Yet another step is to have faith.

In Saint Matthew's account of Jesus' Sermon on the Mount, we find a section that is commonly called the "don't worry passage." I prefer to call it the "workhorse passage." In it, Jesus tells a beautiful story.

As he is giving that sermon, he is standing halfway up one of the rolling hills beside the Sea of Galilee. It is a lovely pastoral scene that has been preserved until this day. As he is standing there, Jesus tells the assembled people to look up.

There are birds swooping and darting through the air, as there are today. Jesus reminds the people that those birds don't sow or reap, or store up food in barns. Instead, they flit about all day looking for the food that God has provided for them. Jesus asks his listeners:

> *If God takes care of the birds of the air, how much greater care will he take of you?*

So we need to have faith, a kind of faith that God, or the higher power you believe in, will intercede and keep watch over us.

I want to stress again that we cannot be passive and sit by complaining, expecting God to appear and protect us from harm. Like my actor friend, we need to take action on our own behalf, so that God can meet us halfway and partner with us as a good shepherd. Even birds are not passive. They know innately that they cannot sit by waiting for food to drop at their feet. They fly up into the air and look about, taking action on their own behalf. In taking that action, they gain the momentum and perspective to move their lives ever forward without the burden of worry or despair. We can do the same in our own lives.

Worry has no place in a life of happiness and success. We need to be active and joyful as we move our lives ahead.

Still another cure for worry is to ask the "what-if" question.

My wife, who is truly remarkable in that she is a person who does not worry, was facing enormous challenges in her business last year. When I asked her what she does to keep herself free from worry, she answered, "I ask the 'what-if' question." She asks, *"What if the worst possible thing that could happen, happened?"*

That is a vital question that can help restore perspective and really put worry in its place. What if everything you are worried about did indeed occur? What if the worst really happened? You will realize that you would know just what to do, that you would have the resources to handle it.

My wife told me one other remarkable thing about asking the what-if question. "After I see that I can handle the worst thing that could happen, I do something else. I trust."

There it is again—the importance of faith in chasing worrying away.

Some years ago, I learned vital lessons about what it means to trust from a young European woman named Josianne who lived with my family and took care of my sons. Now Josianne possessed more absolute, undeniable, pure faith than anybody I have ever known. When she prayed, she would direct the whole energy of her prayer to God, knowing God would answer.

I arrived at my church one Sunday morning, and I found Josianne sitting near my office with her head bowed. She had just returned from a weekend visit to some friends in upstate New York. She had arrived on a bus at the Port Authority Bus Terminal in Manhattan and gone to the ladies' room, leaving her purse outside the stall. It was an act of naïveté that could be committed only by a person new to New York. While she was in the stall, the purse was taken. She asked me to take her to the bus terminal after church to try to find it.

Before the service began, I tried to give her some tips on life in New York. "Forget it," I said. "This is New York! You will never get your purse back. It's gone for good."

Josianne responded, "I am going to pray to God, and I am going to get my purse back!"

During the service, she sat in the balcony. I'd look up on occasion and see her deep in prayer.

It was midafternoon by the time we got to the Port Authority, where we spoke to a police officer. We gave him our names and described the problem. He smiled.

"No wonder I can't get you at home on the phone," he said. "You're here! We found your purse."

This is the power of trust, trust in some higher power. She knew that if she trusted, God would in some way answer her prayer. It happened for her time and time again. I don't think I ever saw her worried. She trusted so much. Josianne had found a way to live without fear, without that insidious demon, worry. She relaxed and got perspective. She took whatever action she needed to. But she also prayed, knowing with certainty that whatever was best for her would happen.

Deepening Our Understanding

What benefits await us once we have broken worry's hold on our lives? I have seen remarkable changes in people's lives, immediate and powerful transformations, once the worry cycle is broken. It can be an astonishing transformation, much like the life change experienced by Ebenezer Scrooge the morning after the three spirits had visited him. Now Scrooge was not a worrier per se; he was a miser and a cruel man. Still, in Dickens's remarkable story of Scrooge, we see an account of the kind of elation we can feel when a burdensome, self-imposed weight is suddenly lifted from us. We feel light, joyful, and empowered to reconnect with our dreams, our hopes, our loved ones. Some might even say that, by shedding worry, we reconnect with our true selves—who we really are:

- *We rediscover what is most important in our lives.* The clouds clear as negativism vanishes.

- *Our friendships and loving relationships are healed.* Our happiness becomes magnetic to others.

- *Success grows because we can again move forward with our careers and other plans.* We can take risks and make decisions without burdens of worry.

- *Our self-esteem and sense of worth soar. "I can, I can . . ."* *replaces "I cannot, I cannot . . ."* We immediately free ourselves to get much more out of living.

- *We reconnect with what is most important in our lives.* Our families, ambitions, and friends regain their rightful, most valued place in the rich mosaic of our lives. Perspective and balance are ours again as we simply enjoy life more.

We really can break worry's hold on our lives. We can do it by admitting our worry problem, taking action on it, having faith, and considering the what-if question. Those are potent steps that, once taken, can chase worry away, make life joyful again, and put us back in control of where our lives are heading.

2

Freedom Follows Making Peace with the Past

When we are children, we feel full of promise and possibility. Then, before we realize it, we arrive at an age when we are looking back at our lives. We see things we wish we had done and things we wish we hadn't done. We see roads not taken. With the wrong orientation and attitude, we could say, "If only I could start my life again today, I would do it all so differently." Or we could say, "If only certain things hadn't happened to me, I would be in a different place today."

Such thoughts are natural. We all have them. Yet when we let them gain too much power over us, past disappointments cripple us and our future. Each day is a new beginning, a new page where we can write any story we choose—new successes, new progress, new wonders. Our ability to do that hinges on how efficient we are at making peace with the past.

I would like to include here the text of a letter I received a few years ago from a member of the Marble Collegiate Church. She is a woman who has been through a lot. Some of the damage she has suffered along the way is so great that her wounds seem to be open and her scars large. Yet she is very much in the process of growing.

Dear Arthur,
Leaving church this afternoon, I noticed your sermon topic for this coming Sunday: "How to Overcome a Difficult Past." A flood of issues came to mind, some of which I thought you might find helpful. . . .

My earliest memories are of severe abuse and neglect. For example, I remember being left alone day after day at age 2 in the playground of a housing project and the things that happened to me as a result of being unattended there. As a result of the first 20 years of my life, I've spent a lifetime struggling to discern truth. I've had to overcome many issues and am still engaged in the process.

I was well into my thirties before I realized that my concept of God was that of an unreliable, untrustworthy, and punitive figure; but that God may be none of these things and that I had confused Him with my early experience of authority figures. Unfortunately, this lack of trust runs deep and presents a major roadblock to developing a strong faith and trust in God.

In my first Sunday at Marble, I heard the startling and simultaneously painful and beautiful message that I am precious in the eyes of God. I am still trying to believe this. Throughout my lifetime, a deep pain has often resurfaced. At such times, I've found it necessary to choose forgiveness again and again in regard to people and events I thought I'd already forgiven and resolved. . . . Even in my middle years, it's still difficult to dream big enough dreams and to discover my purpose in God's plan, and this is my greatest pain.

Life has been very hard for this wonderful woman, yet she is deeply committed to the process. She's dealing with issues, going through counseling, asking the right questions, and associating with fellow seekers.

Life can be a process of profound growth if we trust that some higher being, some greater force, is there with us. If we do, we will rise up to the bigness, the full measure of our growth.

One of the best stories about what happens to people who cannot turn from the past and start a new life can be found in the Book of Genesis. I am speaking about the story of Sodom and Gomorrah. You surely recall the tale of these two cities, destroyed by God because of the evil ways of the people who lived in them.

The Bible tells us that before the cities were destroyed, God decided to save Lot and his wife. They were a righteous people who lived in Sodom, and God saw no reason for them to perish because of the sins of others. So God gave Lot some very specific instructions on how he and his wife could escape. They could leave the city, but God also warned that once they had gone, they had to keep going, without ever looking back.

Once they were outside the city proper, Lot's wife stopped. I believe that she wanted one last look at the past she was leaving behind, which is a natural human tendency. But as soon as she looked back, she was immediately turned into a pillar of salt. Now, the image of a pillar of salt is truly a remarkable one. Yet its significance as a parable is clear. When we drag the past along with us, especially a bad past, we become like statues, literally frozen in place.

I have known many people who have become crippled by the past. They are not all exactly alike, of course, but I think you will recognize many people who share traits like these:

- They are unable to participate fully in the present, or enjoy it. Somehow they cannot completely see all the good things life places before them. Children, security, health, and material possessions all take on secondary significance to a past that was somehow unhappy.

- They cannot learn from past setbacks, only relive them time and time again. I think that most of us now understand that we need to use problems as opportunities to learn and grow. People who have become slaves to their pasts cannot do that. Past problems are not put to good use, only used as scripts that predict greater defeats in the future.

- They become embittered and disliked. Nobody likes to spend time around people who spend all their energy reliving past problems and talking about defeat. This is why dwelling in the past in the wrong way often results in alienation and loneliness.

- They become crippled by remorse. Often their regrets take the shape of "if-only" statements: "If only I had worked harder in high school, I might have gotten into a really good college" or "If only I hadn't married the wrong person the first time around and lost so much time in an unhappy marriage." All those statements get woven together into an image of a grim future that the individual is powerless to control.

- They get caught in the blame cycle, pinning responsibility for past problems on other people. Their parents, wives, bosses, partners, and children would seem to all be involved in a complex conspiracy designed to do personal harm to them. Blame flies all around like a cruel flame, and rational questions of personal responsibility for past problems rarely come into play.

- They often veer into self-abusive, self-destructive patterns. Often they turn to alcohol and other vices that falsely promise relief from past sorrows and regret.

When people ask me, "Will I ever be able to overcome the difficulty of my past?" I have an answer: Yes! Yes, you can overcome the difficulties of your past, no matter how troubling they might be. There is nothing that is not "overcome-able" if you keep the faith, if you never give up and stay with the process of living. The past is behind us. It is not possible for you or I, or any human being, to go back and amend it. We all know this fact, but sometimes we need to be reminded of it, that it is futile to waste our time even worrying about it. The place to start is to learn to think about the past, but to do so in a positive, learning, and action-oriented way.

What can we do to take control of and master this basic human tendency, the tendency to let our futures be controlled by negative events from our pasts?

Learn lessons from the lives of people who have gone beyond difficult pasts to build brilliant futures.

Luckily, we have many examples of individuals who have shown the ability to do just that. Rather than dwelling in defeat and disappointment, they moved forcefully ahead. Such people, if we stop to consider them, serve like bright beacons for us, lighting the way to achieve great things.

Surely, Abraham Lincoln was such a person. In school, we learn that he was one of the greatest presidents and leaders of all time. But we generally don't learn how much he suffered on his way up, starting during his childhood.

> In 1816, when he was still a young boy, his family was forced out of their home. Young Abe went to work to support them.

> In 1818, his mother died.

> In 1832, Abe ran for the Illinois State Legislature and lost badly. He then decided he wanted to go to law school, but he tried and couldn't get in.

> In 1833, he borrowed some money from a friend and started a new business. It failed, and by the end of that year, he was bankrupt and in such debt, it took him another 17 years to pay it off.

> In 1834, he ran for the Illinois State Legislature again. This time, he won.

> In 1835, he became engaged to be married, but his fiancée died.

> In 1836, he apparently suffered a nervous breakdown and was in bed for 6 months.

In 1838, he tried to become speaker of the Illinois State Legislature and was defeated.

In 1843, he ran for the United States Congress and lost.

In 1846, he ran again. This time he won and went to Washington.

In 1848, he ran for reelection to Congress but lost.

In 1849, he applied for the job of land officer in Illinois, which wasn't a very big job, but his application was turned down.

In 1854, he again ran for the U.S. Senate and again lost.

In 1856, he sought the vice presidential nomination at his party's national convention and did not get enough votes.

In 1858, he ran for the U.S. Senate. Again, he lost.

In 1860 he ran for president of the United States, and almost miraculously, he won.

I wonder if his greatness would have been as phenomenal if he had not faced so many hardships, losses, and defeats. Obviously, he did not allow his past to drag him down or failure and misfortune to defeat him. Abraham Lincoln found a way to reinvent himself time and again. He was a person who knew how to make peace with his past and move on.

If we are unlike Lincoln, if we let ourselves be defeated by past problems, how much of our potential is not being expressed? How much of our potential is certain to perish with us?

Every day, remind ourselves that each day offers the promise of a new beginning.

I remember that the first time I heard that phrase, a new light seemed to go on inside me. Before then, I had seen life in compartments. I hadn't seen the grand flow of it. But now I see that every time something finishes, something new begins. Yesterday is gone, but today is always with us. What a powerful concept that can be if we dedicate ourselves to putting it to use.

I would like to share a powerful story with you. It has made such a difference in my life that I keep coming back to it.

On the first Sunday in May 1985, at the request of the Dutch Consulate, we had a celebration service in Marble Collegiate Church to commemorate the fortieth anniversary of Holland's liberation from the Nazi regime.

It was quite a day. We had banners everywhere. Among our visitors were pilots who had made food drops over Holland, and also some of the farmers who had received that food. Tears were shed. It was highly emotional. There were Christians and Jews— a whole wonderful mix of people.

At a luncheon afterward, I was sitting next to a woman about 60 years of age, a woman with a handsome, lovely countenance. Yet I could tell from the deep lines in her face that she had experienced a difficult life.

When I asked her to tell me her story, I learned about her painful past. She said, "When I was 16 years old, I was sent to a Nazi concentration camp. My whole family was there as well. From the chimneys, I saw the smoke representing the bodies of every single one of my family members who had died in the furnaces. I was the only one left.

"On the day of liberation, when they opened the gates of the camp, I owned only the clothing on my back. As I walked down that road away from the camp, I knew I had a decision to make. I could spend the rest of my life hating and cursing those who had done so much harm to my family and to me. Or I could be happy.

"I chose happiness. I decided I was going to have a good life."

She told me that not one day or night has passed when she has not had some horrendous memory or nightmare about those 4 years. But she chose a happy life. And if that choice was available to her, with her difficult past, it is surely available to all of us as well.

Remember, life is not supposed to be easy, but packed with challenges that offer us great opportunities for spiritual growth.

When we take a look at the Bible, we see there is not one word, phrase, paragraph, or chapter that says, "You can relax. Life is going to be easy." In fact, the Bible is filled with countless stories about people who have triumphed over difficult pasts.

The Bible could quite accurately carry the subtitle: "The Book of Overcomers."

Consider Moses. Moses was a great leader. Yet he experienced hardship from his earliest days. He had a speech impediment and depended on his brother to be his spokesperson. When he was a young man, he became enraged, and, like the worst people we read about in our newspapers today, Moses killed someone and hid the body. Yet God raised up Moses to be the leader of his people, whom Moses delivered out of slavery. Moses did not buckle to his difficult past.

Consider Joseph too, that well-known man with the many-colored coat. Unlike Moses, Joseph enjoyed a life that was full of ease, at least in his earliest years. He was born into a loving home. His parents doted on him and believed he was the most wonderful child who had ever existed. But then trouble started. Joseph's brothers all resented the attention he was getting. They became insanely jealous. They decided to kill their brother. But instead, they left him to be sold to a passing caravan and broke their father's heart by telling him that Joseph had been killed by a wild animal. Yet Joseph, too, became a leader of his people. What would have happened if he had caved in to the difficulties in his past?

So it is in the Bible, the Book of Overcomers. It is an inspiring chronicle of people who did not buckle under the weight of their difficult pasts but instead went on to triumph.

We can stay in touch and connected to our growth.

In other words, we can constantly remain in touch with the fact that we are growing with every day. As yesterday passes away and today arrives, we are involved in a powerful process. A small reminder of this fact can be helpful. Make a little sign on your mirror that says, "Today I will grow," or make it a personal reminder that you place on your desk or even in your pocket.

Remember that life is a gift.

Rejoice, claim its riches, and don't be caught up by the bad things. Of course, adopting this outlook can be difficult. But isn't it really a matter of faith and choice? You can decide whether to live a life that remains stuck in past problems, or you can make a new beginning today. It is a choice that no one can make but you.

Deepening Our Understanding

When we think about the past in a positive way, we add richness and perspective to our lives. In contrast, getting stuck and not getting beyond regrets and disappointments is anything but healthy. We actually cripple our ability to move forward with our lives or enjoy each new day.

Instead, we can commit ourselves to building a productive relationship with the past, even if our pasts were difficult or especially troubled. One way is to remember the examples of top achievers and leaders who refused to let defeat cripple them. Every day, we can also remember that we have been given a new gift we can use to make a new beginning.

Growth is the key—staying oriented toward growth. When we commit ourselves to that upward path in life, remarkable things can take place:

- *We live in the present.* We are full of possibility and potential, just as we were when we first came into the world. All the things that surround us bring us more joy.

- *We commit ourselves to what has been called "continuous improvement."* Instead of allowing past difficulties to become crippling self-definitions, we learn all we can from every experience life has brought us. This is a path that can not only make us happy but can make us truly, truly extraordinary in all we do.

- *We become happier.* Surely, happiness is not an insignificant thing! A life lived without the shadow of bitterness is truly a bright jewel, worth working toward.

- *We see troubled relationships healed and rewarding new friendships begin.* Nobody likes to spend time around embittered people who have become mired in the past. But people *do* like to be in the company of people like the one you surely are: positive, full of plans, full of new ideas—full of *life*.

3

Freedom Follows Accepting Pain

---

*W*e would all like life to be free of pain and misfortune. What a life that would be! We'd never have aches and pains or other health problems. We'd never suffer disappointments in love, never see cherished friendships turn sour, and never experience conflict with our parents or children. Death would never rob us of the presence of people we love. Life would be one happy, painless event from start to finish.

Of course, life cannot be like that because pain is a central part of the human experience, a pivotal part of being alive. Because pain cannot be avoided, we have a choice to make about the way we live our lives. We can bristle and balk at life's troubles and say, "This is not fair. I am a victim. This is not the way it is supposed to be in my life!" Or we can learn to see pain for what it really is: a master teacher that can refine us, lift us higher, and make our lives truly extraordinary.

One morning several years ago, I joined a good friend for breakfast. When the waiter approached our table, he looked at me and said, "I know you."

I studied his face. I didn't remember ever seeing him before. But from the moment I met him, I was immediately drawn to him. I could sense that his life had not been easy. I could feel there was a profound ache in his heart.

"How do you know me?" I asked.

"I see you on television on Sunday," he replied.

We started to talk, and, in a few minutes, he told me about his life.

"I've got to tell you something," he said. "For most of my life, I didn't believe in anything. Nothing of that religious stuff made any sense to me . . ."

And he paused to take a breath before resuming.

". . . until I lost my 11-year-old son. After my little boy died, I didn't know what to do. I could have done some crazy things. But I went to faith. I went to God. And I became a believer."

"What was it that made you go to God?" I asked.

"It was the pain," he replied.

The pain, awful and unthinkable though it must have been for a parent who had lost a child, had taken this courageous man to a higher level. He had not run from his pain, he had not taken an easy out. He had done the most difficult work imaginable, and in the end, he had come to live life more deeply.

We don't like to think about the kind of pain that poor man suffered. Yet we can learn a lesson from him. When even the direst despair gets a hold on us, we have the opportunity to go to that higher plane, that higher power.

Life is full of setbacks and pain. In fact, from a certain perspective, each of our lives could be characterized as a running inventory of painful experiences. I have suffered health problems. I have had health crises, often painful ones. My first marriage ended in a difficult divorce. But I am not unusual. When you consider your own life story, you are sure to end up with a similar list of painful experiences.

Yet common as pain is, we cannot let it become our self-definition. We cannot come to see ourselves as nothing more than victims of pain. People who do that inflict irreparable damage to themselves:

- *They feel themselves to be "singled out," personally victimized by the pain of life.* When a person concludes that the fates have singled him or her out for tragedy, life takes on a downward trajectory. The sufferer cannot see any way out of the undertow of misfortune that is pulling ever downward.

- *Pain and suffering become the link the person uses to connect to the world.* Talk with friends, which should be uplifting, becomes just an outer rehashing of pain, wrongs done, and disappointments. In fact, all experiences that should be uplifting and positive—from going to church to visiting a helpful counselor or physician—center not on healing but on the particulars of that person's problems. Pain becomes like a pair of dark sunglasses that diminishes and dims every bright thing the person sees.

- *Relationships suffer erosion and irreparable harm.* No one likes to spend time in the company of people who can talk about little else except how much life has caused them to suffer.

- *The sufferer falls victim to false authorities and ineffective remedies.* People who feel themselves to be victims of life are often the most likely to become involved with shallow, short-term authorities—from cult religions to self-promoting gurus to false friends who offer self-serving advice and counsel. Instead of reaching out for the wisdom of the ages, which tells that hard work is required to process and understand life's pain, they run from one authority to another, seeking short-term results.

If regret and pain have gained a firm hold on your life, how can you begin to turn the situation around?

Stop thinking like a victim, and learn to see pain as an invitation to growth.

Some of us, in response to pain, become deeper, wiser, more compassionate human beings. Others among us grow shallower, shorter on understanding and smaller in character.

Why do only some of us grow in response to pain while others do not? I believe it is because some of us have learned to grow so that we gain from life's difficult experiences, while others haven't. How can we become deeper through pain? We can begin by considering these three don'ts:

- *Don't try to run from pain.* Trying to run from pain won't work. Pain is part of living. If you try to run from it, you only increase its power over you. Eventually it will overtake you and engulf your life. One day, it might even defeat you.

- *Don't curse pain.* It is difficult, but vital, to remember that the distress you are feeling might contain the very seed of the remedy that you need to catapult you to new growth, learning, wisdom, understanding, patience, and depth of character.

- *Don't go looking for pain.* In response to pain, it's amazing how many people go right back and back into situations that they recognize are damaging and wounding. They are drawn back time and again to the same kinds of negative friends, difficult relationships, and impossible jobs—the list could go on and on. So it is vital not to live in the pain, but to move beyond it.

So if those are the don'ts, what are we to do when we find ourselves unable to get past life's difficulties, pain, and disappointments? There is one major lesson to learn.

When you are in pain, face it. Look it straight in the eye. Focus on it. Name it. Understand it.

It is vitally important to trace the pain to its cause so that you can understand the issue or problem you are dealing with. Get to the source of the pain so that you can start to loosen its hold over your life. You can start this process by completing the sentence, "I am in pain because . . ."

Are you hurting because of a broken relationship? Because you are lonely? Because you lost your job? Or perhaps you are hurting because someone said something that injured you deeply?

Even if you have lost a loved one to death, immersing yourself in the pain can begin the healing process. To begin to move past the pain, it's vital to feel the feeling completely, identify it, trace it, and get to the cause.

This is a very sensible approach. Consider the fact that, if you have a stomachache, your doctor and you will focus on your stomach and work to identify the cause of the problem. Your doctor will not look at your big toe or your shoulder but at the origin of the pain. To make things better, the two of you must consider where the discomfort is coming from. Only then can you bring the understanding you need to end the hurt and move past the problem.

Years ago a member of my congregation came to see me, hurting inside because she felt so alone. She told me she felt unable to enter into a close friendship with anyone. We spent time together discussing her problem, trying to understand what lay beneath it. All our talking did not yield the answers she needed. She needed to do her solitary work, alone.

Some time later, she came back to me and said, "Arthur, I think I have gotten to the cause. I have been the problem. I have been so eager to build relationships that when I meet people I like, I hang onto them too tenaciously. I become too demanding and drag the energy right out of them. In the end, I drive them away."

Finally, when things had become substantially happier in her life, she told me, "Arthur, I had to learn to be alone and to face my loneliness before I was in a position to relate to other people."

She had to learn to face her loneliness, get right down to the root of her pain, in order to embark on a new path in her life. That seems logical, doesn't it? Yet we don't often apply this rational approach when we're confronted by troubles. When something hurts, we run away from it. We duck it. We think about everything except the problem we need to be facing. And so often, we don't handle pain well as a result.

I learned this valuable lesson myself when, in a moment of loneliness, I shared my hurt with a friend. He said to me, "Arthur, you have to allow pain its time." That's a psychology of dealing with pain that promotes, not impedes, our growth. The process takes time and cannot be hurried.

One of the master teachers in the area of human growth and suffering was Paul the Apostle. If you have spent time with his writings, you know they emerged from the turmoil and pain in his own life. Paul was a great intellect, but he didn't write from his head. He wrote from his heart and from the very center of his being.

Paul's words teach us profound lessons about how we should handle ourselves when we're afflicted. One piece of his advice has been immensely important for me at times when I have found it difficult to handle the troubles I am in the midst of. Every time I have trusted these words and done the work they demand, they have lifted me higher and higher, out of the depths:

All things work together for good to the person who loves God and who is called according to God's purpose.
—Romans 8:28

Paul is telling us that all the events in our lives, whether joyous or bitter, can be woven into the fabric of our growth. God stands ready to help us use anything and everything that comes to us to make good things happen, even suffering. No experience goes to waste in our lives.

If you trust Paul's words, you can take whatever happens in your life and become reborn as a bigger, fuller, and deeper person.

We can live our lives in just this way. Even when we are facing the harshest loneliness, the deepest pain, the most profound despair, we can find a spiritual power, and rely on it, to turn the negatives into positives. Unless we do that, unless we deal with our pain, we can never experience our fullest growth.

One of my favorite stories illustrating this truth concerns the English botanist Alfred Russell Wallace, who lived about 150 years ago. Every time I tell this story, people say, "I've heard that story before, but today I really heard its message for the first time. Thank you." I hope you find the same depth of meaning in it.

One day in his laboratory, Wallace was observing an Emperor butterfly seeking to get free from its cocoon. The scientist was struck by the little butterfly's painful struggle and the length of time it was pushing and pulling, working to get free. He wondered, "What would happen if I assisted in the process?" And so he took his scalpel and he cut down the length of the cocoon. He watched to see what would happen, and these are his exact words:

The butterfly emerged from the cocoon, spread its wings, drooped perceptibly—and died.

The butterfly needed to struggle. It needed the pain, all that intense work. Otherwise, the juices would not be distributed into every square millimeter of its large, beautiful wings. Without all the pain, there would be no beauty, no color, no character, and no life.

Struggle and pain are necessary to create a beautiful, living creature. We, too, need that effort and work, yet there are people among us who refuse to see the growth potential in struggle.

Dr. Gary Zukav, author of the book *Soul Stories* (Fireside Books, 2000), looks at these questions from a slightly different perspective. He asks how much "digging" we have done in our lives. When unpleasant events have happened, have we dug down to see what we can learn from them, to discern their meaning? Have we dug into our pain until we found the gold? Because when we do that, our lives become like gifts that have been designed especially for us. We need to *dig down* into our pain in order to make it go away.

For its lessons about adversity and pain, I recommend another book too. It is *Further Along the Road Less Traveled* by M. Scott Peck (Touchstone Books, 1998). In this book, the author continues to share insights from the spiritual journey that he began when he wrote *The Road Less Traveled*. Here is what he says about pain:

The quickest way to change your attitude toward pain is to accept the fact that everything that happens has been designed for spiritual growth.

That's quite a statement, that the pain that happens to you is designed for your spiritual advantage. Peck is reminding us that we are not bodies that happen to have souls. We are souls who happen to have bodies. We come from God, and we go to God. We are here on this earth in mortal life with a physical body, with material things to deal with, so that our souls can grow and develop. And pain is a big part of that process.

Deepening Our Understanding

Our pain turns to joy when, with integrity, we stay involved in the difficult process of learning and growing from adversity. If we can stay with that endeavor, we will see remarkable things happen in our lives:

- *We feel a new connection with all members of the human family.* Since we no longer feel ourselves to be "singled out" or victimized by our individual troubles, we begin to feel new connections and commonalities to all people. We can empathize more effectively with other people's life situations and grow into deeper, more caring individuals.

- *We discover new opportunities to take positive action in the world.* Adversity is no longer a block to action in the world but a comrade that deepens our awareness and understanding of life. We become freer and more empowered to achieve more in every area of life, from our loving relationships to our work.

- *We become more open to experiences of love, kindness, and beauty.* Instead of those dark sunglasses mentioned earlier in this chapter—the ones that dim every bright thing that comes before us—we go through life with eyes that are fully open to every good and beautiful thing that we see.

- *Our relationships heal and become deeper.* When people around us sense that we are again involved in the processes of growing and enjoying life, they are drawn to us.

- *We become more active seekers of wisdom.* With the obstacles of bitterness and pain rolled out of the way, we become more open to the wisdom of the ages. With the pain of life in healthy perspective, we are better able to discern the real meanings of faith. In the end, our pain can turn to joy.

4

Freedom Follows Passion

---

*P*assion is a word we don't often use. It seems like an emotion that ought to belong to artists, or musicians, or people in the first stages of falling in love. Yet there is a place for passion in our daily lives. In fact, if we are to live life fully, passion must be moved from the periphery of our lives to the very center. There is no greater force that can empower us to reach our full potential, and experience complete joy, as we engage in the process of living.

On Halloween morning some years ago, I called my 3-year-old granddaughter Isabella. What a joy! She was so excited.

"Are you going trick-or-treating tonight?" I asked.

"Oh, Granddad," she gushed. "I'm going to be a fairy angel. I have a shiny silver skirt, and I'm going to have great big wings, like a fairy butterfly!"

We had an animated conversation about what Halloween night would be like. She told me about her friends, about the pumpkin they had carved, and about the people who would come to their door wearing astonishing costumes. For me, it was a wonderful conversation. I was overwhelmed by it.

Oh, to have the passion, excitement, the thrill of a child's mind! We all had it once. Weren't we all like little Isabella? Passionate, excited, and enthusiastic about everything that was about to take place in our lives?

The fact is that our lives could be surrounded by such passion. So why do some of us seem to be sleepwalking through life, as though we were permanently sedated? One reason is that life can be taxing. Some of us are overwhelmed by its frustrations, hurts, and disappointments. Another reason is that we let other people's opinions affect us. We think, "Well, maybe I'm not supposed to be as passionate. It isn't the thing to do. I've got to tone it down."

Great achievers have set aside that thought pattern where passion is involved. When Thomas Edison was once asked what he believed to be the greatest invention of all time, he answered, "The greatest invention ever is the mind of a child."

We know that Thomas Edison was an adult, a man who achieved astonishing things. He was a scientist, an inventor, and an accomplished leader in business. In light of those accomplishments, we might expect him to be grim, sober, and detached in his personality. The opposite was true. Everything he did, and all his greatness, resulted from his remarkable, childlike enthusiasm.

Later on the same Halloween day that I had spoken with Isabella, I performed a wedding. As is the custom, after the benediction I leaned over to the groom and said, "You may kiss the bride." They kissed and kissed and kissed some more. For a moment I thought I would have to break it up! It was wonderful. After the ceremony, that couple had included an ancient African custom called "jumping the broom." After their extended kiss, the groom laid a broom on the floor. They jumped over it and literally ran down the aisle. Then, seconds later, I heard two loud shrieks from just outside the sanctuary. It was the bride calling out happily, expressing her joy with an extraordinary passion. Oh, to be that passionate about life!

Passion is often absent in our adult lives. Its lack is felt in so many crucial areas of our lives. Without passion:

- *We accept dull routines, dull activities, and dull lives.*
  We miss out on the newness and the adventure of every new day.

- *We miss the real value of the people around us.* All the people around us offer a newness and an excitement that we overlook if passion is gone from our lives.

- *We never tap our creative potential.* As I observed above, artists are often said to possess passion. There is a reason. Without passion, we cannot think in creative new ways. We accept the old, tired, and routine.

- *We lose sight of our own possibilities and potential.* Some years ago, Sammy Davis, Jr., wrote a book about his accomplishments called *Yes I Can!* It was a bestseller when it first appeared and is still selling well in its 1990 edition (Noonday Press). There is a reason for the success of this book, which tells the story of a remarkable man who, without passion, would have become a victim of his own limitations.

- *We miss opportunities to take our lives in important new directions.* We've been trained to think objectively and assess risks before taking risks in our lives. Those are important steps, of course, in minimizing the danger of doing chancy things in our lives. Yet the fact remains that few great things have been accomplished without the fire of passion behind them. We could never build great bridges, write novels, or fall in love without passion.

How then can we rekindle passion in our lives, especially when we have grown older than little Isabella?

We can remember that passion is appropriate, no matter our age.

It may seem as though we lose passion as we get older, but I don't believe passion is age related. Have you recently observed a group of teenagers? Yes, many of them are passionately involved in life and enthusiastic, and yet so often many seem to drag about sullen and bored, as though they have nothing in their lives to be excited about. What a waste! They have youth, health, vigor, and energy. Their whole lives are ahead of them. They can change the world!

Some experts have concluded that the lackluster, lifeless outlook of many young people is a result of the hormonal changes that affect them in those years. There is undoubtedly some truth to that, but I believe it is more a cultural thing. Teenagers observe one another walking about with a detached manner, and they assume it is the best way to be "cool."

But other teenagers are not that way. I certainly wasn't. My teen years were some of the best of my life. I looked forward to life. I was excited. I was into everything. I did a lot of unwise things, yes. That's part of the learning experience. But I was somehow lucky. I never lost enthusiasm.

Of course, enthusiasm can be lost at other points in our lives. We can become disenchanted with life in our early working years, in our middle years, or at other times. We can come to see life as lackluster, boring, and dull. Yet that's not the way it needs to be for everyone, no matter how old he or she is.

We can also remind ourselves that passion can start like a new fire at any time, on any day.

Often, firing up our passion can start with a simple act, the act of reminding ourselves that it is possible to be passionate about our lives. Wherever we are in our lives, we can learn to reconnect with the gift of passion that was with us at birth, that spirit I found in little Isabella.

A friend of mine was once a writer for *Fortune* magazine. She once described an assignment to me. She was to interview a group of Fortune 500 CEOs to determine what they had in common. She found these ultrasuccessful people, by and large, were quite different. Their childhoods had been different. So had their educations and their early jobs. They lived in different areas of the country. They worked in different industries. They practiced different religions. They belonged to different political parties. Their philosophies were not the same. Yet she found that there was one thing they all had in common. It was a passion for what they were doing, a passion for what life is all about.

We can also fire our passion by actively practicing excitement in our daily lives.

I have a friend who was the first cellist with the Metropolitan Opera Orchestra for many years. While there, he played under some of the greatest conductors of our time. I once asked him what makes a great conductor. He said there were a number of things, such as musical knowledge, good people skills, the knowledge to run a rehearsal effectively, and more. He listed many of those practical traits for me. But then he said:

> *The greatest conductors have immense energy . . . an energy that inspires.*

Once again, we encounter passion. And we also discover that passion can be awakened by the act of investing energy and enthusiasm into our daily activities.

Several years ago, I read a wonderful book that was inspiring and helpful to me. It is called *Jesus in Blue Jeans* (Hyperion Books, 1998), written by Laurie Beth Jones, who has also written other fine books on spiritual growth.

Jesus in Blue Jeans includes a segment on passion. As an entry into the discussion, she writes about eight definitions of *passion* from the Random House *Webster's College Dictionary*. It's worth repeating here:

> *Passion: 1. compelling emotion 2. strong amorous feeling; love 3. strong sexual desire; lust 4. A strong fondness, enthusiasm, or desire for something 5. the object of one's passion 6. an outburst of emotion 7. violent anger; wrath; rage 8. the sufferings of Christ on the cross or subsequent to the Last Supper.*

Then she adds:

Every person you see around you is the result of a passion-
ate encounter, as are you and I. Passion is the force that
ensures the creation of new life. It is the essence of creativ-
ity, the heart of strong desire.

We can also connect with the spiritual aspects of passion.

I find it interesting that the *Webster's College Dictionary* definition of *passion* reaches out to encompass the feelings of Christ. Jesus demonstrated God's passionate desire toward us. He described himself as a bridegroom seeking his bride. In describing the marriage rites, he urged us to become "one," using the same term as the "two becoming one flesh" described in the marriage ceremony. He poured his life out in passionate, meaningful encounters with everyone he met. He held nothing back.

So we see that our spiritual lives and beliefs are not staid or noncommittal. They call us to passion-filled lives.

We can reconnect with our purpose in the world.

I have a friend who is the widow of a Methodist minister. A few months after her husband died, she told me she'd been through quite an experience since his death. People had been calling her often, making all sorts of job offers. But she had turned them all down.

"I had to get in touch with myself to see what it was I really wanted to do," she told me. "I discovered that all my life I had been a nurturer, and that is how I want to spend the rest of my life. I'm going to nurture people."

Because she has the passion and because it is her highest good, I know she will do it.

In order to have full lives, lived with passion, we need to consider what our highest good is. As more people consider this question today, many are finding that they may need to consider making less money. Later in this book, we will discuss the importance of considering our relationship to money as we forge new, freer lives. I need to also mention money here, while we are exploring passion. What is money compared to happiness? Money is the means to an end, but we are only wasting time if we let it stand between us and our real life passions.

We can refuse to worry about how we will be perceived when we practice passion and be passionate anyway.

From time to time I think of a story Maya Angelou reports so movingly in her book *Won't Take Nothing for My Journey Now* (Bantam Books, 1994) about a member of her family named Aunt Tee. For many years, Aunt Tee lived in southern California, where she worked for a very wealthy family. Her employers owned a 14-room ranch house and three cars, and they employed a full staff. Aunt Tee was the head of the staff. When she first worked for them, she organized many parties for them, but over time they stopped giving parties. Aunt Tee, however, would still have her own parties every Saturday night. She and her friends would get together and they would laugh. They would tell stories, play cards, sing songs, stomp feet, and be happy.

One of these Saturday nights when Aunt Tee was entertaining her friends, she felt a cool breeze on the back of her neck. She turned around and noticed her employers had opened the door. No, they were not there to ask Aunt Tee to stop having fun. They were there because of something that was lacking in their own lives. One of her employers said to her:

We have been watching you on Saturday nights. Would you mind if we kept watching? There is so much laughter in your room.

What a tragedy! This family had so much, yet they were still lacking that passion that is so vital in life. They had lost the gift of passion that God gives us at birth.

How can we reconnect with our gift of passion, our birthright to it? Laurie Beth Jones suggests that we can do it by reconnecting with our highest good, our natural gift. I think that is a wonderful suggestion. She is reminding us that if we like to sing, we should find a way to sing a song. If we like to dance, we should dance. If we want to write, or start a new company, or paint a painting, we should get off the sidelines and do it. Do it forcefully, with joy and with conviction. Whatever your passion is, get to it and let it change you. Don't worry about what other people say. Don't worry about whether it's right or wrong. Just do it. You'll find that a passionate life quickly becomes a fully dimensioned, joyous experience. A life of rich rewards.

Deepening Our Understanding

Some time ago I came across a poem written by a lady named Nadine Stair when she was 85 years old. It's entitled "If I Had My Life to Live Over." Some might argue that it is not great literature, yet it is reproduced in shortened form in the book *Chicken Soup for the Soul* by Jack Canfield and Mark Victor Hansen (HCI, 1993). I don't care whether it is great literature or not because it contains such valuable lessons on living life with passion. Let me share a shortened version with you here.

> *If I had my life to live over . . .*
> *I'd dare to make more mistakes next time. I'd relax. I would limber up. I would be sillier than I have been this trip. I would take fewer things seriously. I would take more chances. I would take more trips. I would climb more mountains and swim more rivers.*
> *I would eat more ice cream and less beans. I would perhaps have more actual troubles but I'd have fewer imaginary ones. You see, I'm one of those people who live*

sensibly and sanely hour after hour, day after day. Oh, I've had my moments and if I had it to do over again, I'd have more of them. In fact, I'd try to have nothing else. Just moments. One after another, instead of living so many years ahead of each day.

If I had my life to live over, I would start barefoot earlier in the spring and stay that way later in the fall. I would go to more dances. I would ride more merry-go-rounds. I would pick more daisies.

This is what she is saying: "I would be more passionately involved in the things that really count." That is a lesson we would all do well to heed.

5

Freedom Follows
Getting Centered

*L*ast year, a friend of mine began to study the craft of pottery and, in particular, the art of making pots and bowls on a pottery wheel. The first pot she made on the wheel turned out to be deceptively easy. She placed a mound of clay on the center of the wheel, cupped her hands over it as it spun, and then used her fingers to make a hole in the middle and then pull the edges of the clay upward until she had made a pleasing little pot. "This will not be so difficult," she thought.

She did not realize that she had just experienced what is so often called "beginner's luck." Somehow, on her first try, she had centered the clay just right. It took her more than a month to duplicate that first lucky experience. "Once that mound of clay is centered perfectly and running smoothly in your hands as it spins, you can make anything out of it that you want," she told me. "And if the clay is not perfectly centered, there is no rectifying the problem as you try to make your pot. It veers quickly off center the higher it gets, and it finally collapses into an ugly, shapeless mass of clay. The centering is everything."

Our lives are a lot like that. When we are centered and stable and strong, we can go anywhere we want and accomplish what we need to with a sense of freedom and ease.

When I think about getting centered, I always remember the lessons I learned one summer afternoon in Maine. I was a teenager on a ferryboat crossing the bay to the island where my parents had a cottage. The boat was old, narrow, and wooden. If you went to the lower deck, you would see the shiny brass steam-powered pistons, pumping away. On the upper deck, a canopy protected people from the elements. Today, that boat would be considered an antique. Then, it was basic transportation.

Since it was late on a Friday afternoon, the boat was crowded, standing room only. Then as we steamed down the bay, the wind suddenly whipped up, and a hard rain began, driving at an angle under the canopy. The people on the rainy side quickly moved to the opposite side, and as they did, the boat started to list. Sensing danger, everyone instinctively moved toward the center, and the boat immediately righted itself.

This is a good analogy for the need we human beings have to be centered. Out of centeredness comes stability. And from stability, a more meaningful life experience. We are more in control, freer to move our lives in any direction we like without being blown about by forces that are outside our control.

The dictionary defines *stability* as "the ability to withstand force or stress without alteration of position and without material change." Wouldn't you like to have that kind of balance? In facing both normal daily stresses and exceptional challenges, you could calmly withstand the force or stress without being thrown around.

What happens when you are not centered? When your boat is listing to the right or the left or when we are like that mound of potter's clay that spins off-center and cannot be controlled?

- *You lose all sense of ease and flow in your activities.* When you are centered, difficult tasks seem easy because you are operating from an internal core of balance and strength. Without that center, the opposite is true: Easy tasks seem difficult. As a result, it becomes much more difficult to move your life in the direction you desire. Do you intend to become a musician, to teach school, or to start a company? Such goals become vastly more difficult to reach when you have lost control over the direction of your life by being uncentered.

- *A negative momentum can take hold over you, spinning your life still further off center.* At first, small events seem unsettling. You feel upset and out of control over even small irritations. We let the traffic jams and minor annoyances of daily life get to us, and then, before we know it, we lose our ability to deal calmly with life's greater challenges. It can become an increasing challenge to regain a sense of calm control over more important issues present in our relationships, careers, and finances. Uncentered people feel as though they are living their lives at the control of external events and forces.

Clearly, an uncentered life poses many frustrating problems, including a lack of achievement and an overall lack of joy. How can we get our lives back on center?

We can focus on what is most important to us.

Not long ago, I came across a story that is really a parable on just this principle. In this tale, a wealthy industrialist comes upon a fisherman who is relaxing beside his boat on the bank of a river, puffing on his pipe. The industrialist is annoyed by the man's apparent laziness.

"Why aren't you out there fishing?" he demands to know.

"I've already been fishing, and I've got all the fish I need."

"Why don't you go out and fish for some more?"

"What would I do with them?" the man asks.

"Why, you could sell them and buy a motor for your boat. Then you could take it out into deeper waters and get even more fish. With the money you made, you could buy more nets and bring in even more fish. With all the money you'd earn, you could buy another boat. Maybe one day you'd own a whole fleet of boats, and you'd be wealthy like me! Then you could do anything you want."

And the fisherman replied, "What do you think I'm doing right now?"

That fisherman is a man with a sense of self. Unlike him, most of us are listing a bit to the right and the left, trying to get centered by juggling too many peripheral considerations at the same time. How can we avoid that? I believe that the place to go to find your center is deep within yourself.

We can locate our inner center of calm and peace, and we can commit ourselves to "visiting" that place often.

Much of life is an interior journey. Do we not spend most of our time reflecting on ideas, feelings, memories, dreams, and expectations? We have such an active life inside. But can we get to the center?

Thomas Kelly, the noted Quaker writer, described our center as "the inner sanctuary of the soul." Can we arrive at that place, the inner sanctuary of our soul? If we could, we would discover a quiet place, a place of extraordinary peace.

The Bible makes numerous references to our need to find peace and stillness. One good example is Psalm 46, verse 10. I think I quote this verse more than any other in the Bible because it's so central to spirituality. Also, I personally need so much to hear these words:

Be still and know that I am God.

Please take a moment and read those words once more. God is in all the activities of our busy lives. But at God's deepest and most profound, God is in the stillness.

Then, in Psalm 23, the psalmist asks God to lead him beside the still waters. There is something special about bodies of water. There is an energy in water that draws us to it and calms us. The psalmist describes the effect of the still waters as restoring his soul. That psalm is all about finding peace and getting centered.

We can see ourselves as spiritual beings on a human journey.

Of all the ideas that have had a major impact on my life, perhaps the greatest of them comes from Teilhard de Chardin, a great humanist and religious thinker who lived from 1881 until 1955. He tells us that most of us see ourselves as human beings on a spiritual journey, human beings trying to find God, when the reverse is true. We really are spiritual beings on a human journey. And we're not satisfied, our thirst is not quenched, until we reconnect with who we really are and get in touch with something spiritual.

We can recognize the spiritual, even religious, nature of our daily lives.

Becoming quiet is one of the most effective ways to connect with the spiritual presence in our lives, because quiet is an internal state that is available to us whenever and wherever we are.

Not too long ago, a friend lent me a tape that she said had helped her achieve that kind of connection through the process of visualization. I was skeptical, but I listened to the tape and found that its advice—to visualize a peaceful place at busy times and "visit" it mentally—really does have a calming, centering effect on me.

In my case, I decided to recall a very favorite place of mine on an island off the coast of Maine. I conjured up memories of one very special time I had experienced there. It was an early morning, and I had walked out to a place on the beach. There I sat by myself, smelling the wonderful ocean smells, marveling at the white pure sand, wondering at the water on that particular day, so still yet, so powerful.

I tried to recall that moment as clearly as I could. And I was surprised to find that after that, I was able to revisit it. I could go back to that place to become centered, calm, and in touch with something greater than myself.

We can keep pursuing the goal of being calm and balanced even when we feel ourselves pulled off center.

Recently I came across a delightful little book called *Every Day Sacred: A Woman's Journey Home* by Sue Bender (Harper Books, 1996). In it, she writes about the beauty and sacredness in the ordinary events of life. In her book, she tells the story of a friend who went on vacation with her husband to a national park. One day, while riding a bicycle there, this friend fell and hurt her knee. But since she and her husband had plans to take a hike that day, she decided she would go ahead and take the hike anyway. Because she couldn't walk very fast and had to rest frequently, she had a series of transforming experiences. She began to see the beautiful in the ordinary. She watched a battle between a lizard and a centipede in which the centipede tried to protect itself by stinging the lizard and the lizard nimbly evaded the sting. She also spent long moments looking at unusual, beautiful wild flowers.

At one point, she noticed that there was a hiker with a camera on the trail behind her. Then she noticed that each time she moved along, this other hiker would move up and take a photograph of what she had just been looking at. When she asked him about it, he told her, "You see the most beautiful things, and you've helped me to see them too."

And she said, "I see them because I can't walk very fast."

Now, here in the hustle and bustle of life in New York City (and in the similar hustle and bustle where else we live), we tend to do everything too rapidly. We need to settle down and get quiet. Not walk so fast. We need to find that still point in the midst of activity. Finding that still place is much more likely if we make a personal commitment to that quest.

We can actively seek out silence.

When troubles strike us, what do most of us do? We turn up the volume, don't we? We don't seek silence. We go to loud places to distract ourselves and take our minds off our problems.

When we turn up the noise that way, we're refusing to face our problems. We're refusing to face ourselves. The racket becomes a protection, a defense.

If we're ever going to get in touch with problems and deal with them effectively, we need to face them in quiet and live with them for a time.

Are there practical ways to do that, despite all the noise and hectic pace of our lives? Yes, there are.

First, we can set aside quiet time to get in touch with ourselves. A number of years ago, a man who was widely recognized as one of America's greatest marketing geniuses told me the story of a turning point in his life.

After he finished college, he moved to New York, where he wanted to make it big. He started by taking jobs at several companies to gain the knowledge and experience he needed. Then, when he felt he was ready, he started his own firm.

As his company began to take off, he hired more and more employees. He was doing very, very well. He bought an expensive house in an exclusive part of Westchester County, north of New York City. He was a successful businessman, and very busy.

The turning point in his life came during a visit to his parents' family farm in Indiana. They were all sitting around the kitchen table, warmed by an old stove, enjoying a home-cooked meal of meat, potatoes, fresh vegetables, and homemade pie.

He was telling his parents, very proudly, how busy he was and how well he was doing. He declared, "I get up at 5 a.m. every morning. I shave, I shower, and I'm on the 6:30 train into the city!"

He told them about all his meetings, luncheons, and dinners and about all the important people he knew. How busy he was!

They were quiet for a moment. And then his father said, "Son, I want to ask you a question."

He said, "What is it, Dad?"

His father said, "When do you think?"

After a pause, he replied, "Dad, I've never considered that before."

His father was on target. His son had eliminated every fragment of quiet time from his life. His life was like a hurricane, but he had no center, no core, no eye.

He resolved that when he went back to New York, he would do something different. Keeping that promise to himself, he made some profound changes in his life, and he stuck to them for the rest of his 30-year career.

Each day he would go to the office, take care of administrative duties, read the mail, and dictate his responses. But then he closed the door and shut off the phones. For up to an hour every morning, he would be quiet to think, ponder, and contemplate.

Later on, when he got further along on his spiritual journey, he used that quiet time for prayer. That silent time, he told me, had become the most important part of his day.

We, too, can achieve a quiet heart by setting aside time each day to withdraw from the noise and hubbub. Away from the noise, we can get in touch with the deeper rhythms of life.

We can simplify our lives.

This is a lifelong challenge for all of us, especially in this modern world with its ever-increasing pace and change.

I would like to recommend another excellent book, *Simple Abundance: A Daybook of Comfort and Joy* by Sarah Breathnach (Warner Books, 1995). In it, Ms. Breathnach offers some effective suggestions for coping with stress and getting centered. Here are some of her fine ideas:

- *Carve out an hour a day for solitude.*
- *Begin and end the day with prayer, meditation, and reflection.*
- *Keep your life simple. Don't overschedule it.*
- *Never make a promise you can't keep.*
- *Breathe—deeply and often.*
- *Laugh more often.*

- *Stop trying to please everybody.*
- *Express love every day.*
- *Search for your authentic self until you find him or her.*

The number of people applying this kind of thinking to simplify their lives is growing. Perhaps on some subconscious level, they understand that it is time to get centered in their lives. It's an idea I urge you to consider too.

We can reconnect with sources of true, enduring wisdom.

For many centuries, a large part of the world has been influenced by a few short paragraphs known as the *Ten Commandments*. These rules for living can center us, and they can also steady and stabilize us. When we violate them, we violate ourselves and others and accordingly complicate our lives. Following the Ten Commandments is a way of simplifying life and moving toward being centered.

Let us look at only a few of them in that light:

"Love God with all your heart, mind, soul, and strength."
This is the simplest advice of all. Focus on God. Focus on the divine. This centers you on the most elementary and essential relationship of your life.

Then we come to the "thou shalt nots" of the Ten Commandments, which are really instructions to us about ways to eliminate negative actions that unnecessarily complicate life.

"Don't steal."   We have no right to what belongs to others, even though we try to justify it sometimes. Stealing is wrong. When we do it, we pull ourselves seriously off center and set off a chain of events over which we have absolutely no control.

"Don't kill."   Nobody has the right to take another person's life. Life is the most sacred thing. Everybody loses when one kills another.

"Don't commit adultery."   Today, we live in permissive times. But adultery remains a life-breaker. It breaks up relationships, families, and communities. It never works. People want to make it work, and often they say that it "feels right," but it never really works. It wreaks destruction and tears lives apart.

"Don't bear false witness."   Don't say things that are not true and that will destroy another's reputation and place in the community. We all know how complicated life can become when we begin to say negative things about our neighbors and friends, even in idle gossip.

"Don't covet."   Don't keep longing for what you don't have. Don't envy somebody else because they have something you want. Your life will be simpler and more serene if you are simply content with your own possessions.

When we live in the way of the Ten Commandments, we simplify so much of life, and we stay centered.

We can choose to pray or engage in a regular period of spiritual reflection.

I urge you to find a way to contact God in a quiet time each day. There are fewer more effective or practical ways to get centered.

Over the centuries, many mystics have said that when we pray, we need to say only one word: God. So as you sit silently and get quieter and quieter, I urge you to say that word over and over again: God. God. God.

What will happen if you try this experiment? Much of the time, what we often call "the peace of God, which passes all understanding" begins to take hold. You will get centered. You will become focused. And then you will feel that you are becoming stabilized. You will get in touch with the spiritual power that is within you.

I have my own personal ritual that involves silence. Toward the end of every August, when my wife and I are in Maine, I get up in the middle of the night, get into my little boat, and take it out as far as I can. I go 15 or 20 miles out to where I can no longer see land. Then I turn off the engine, face the eastern sky, and wait for the sunrise.

If you have never seen a sunrise over the ocean, I commend the experience to you. It will be a holy, magnificent, transcendent experience for you.

I sit there in the boat. Everything is absolutely quiet, except for the lapping of water against the bow. Then in the eastern sky, a ribbon of pink appears. As the time of dawn comes closer and closer, the pink becomes concentrated and grows darker and deeper. Then, when the sun rises, it doesn't just glide up. It bursts up over the horizon.

One time, the dawn seemed so dramatic to me that I stood up at attention as tears ran down my cheeks. Extraordinary! Each time I experience the dawn in this way, I sense that I am present at creation. It is the birth of a new day, and the most magnificent part of it all is that the day is born in absolute silence, stillness, and quiet.

We see that the cosmos is not chaos. There's unity. There's harmony.

We can observe a personal sabbath or quiet day each week.

There was a time when people took a day off each week, a sabbath. Even people who were not religious took a day away from their work and regular routines. Today, stores are open every day. Sunday comes, but it is no different from all the other days of the week. And we're all the losers.

We're spiritual beings, and we need some kind of ritual of quiet in our lives, even if that means taking only a day a week to reconnect with our spiritual side and get centered. Didn't God say after the world was created:

I was tired. I rested on the seventh day.

We can engage in calm reflection before life's bigger challenges.

We know that Jesus often went into silence to become still and centered as a way of preparing for major events. He claimed time away from other people. He went to quiet, lonely places where he could be alone. In that quiet, he was able to get in touch with himself and with God.

We can actively seek out the right pace for our lives.

How often do we think about pacing today? Very rarely. Yet each person has a pace that's just right for him or her. Some of us are like race horses. Some of us are like tortoises. Between those two extremes, we can find the tempo of life that embodies just the right tension, the right speed, the sense of movement that's best for us. Even in very busy times, we can still control our pace. How much more centered our lives become when we do so.

Life, with its difficulties and complexities, continually tests us. That is why it benefits us to go to that quiet place where we will not be knocked down or thrown around, where we can get centered and stabilized. That place of stillness, we know, is our spiritual center.

Deepening Our Understanding

In today's world, we often feel surrounded by events that are spinning out of control. The path of least resistance seems to be to spin along too, allowing ourselves to be blown further off center with each unsettling new event or destabilizing force.

Yet another road lies open before us, a more controlled and rewarding one, when we decide to apply some of the steps I suggest in this chapter by finding stillness, connecting with real wisdom, simplifying our lives, and observing a personal sabbath. With these steps, we glimpse a new horizon where we are empowered to:

- *Remain calm in the face of life's small annoyances.* With your center strong, minor frustrations cannot pull you or your mood off base. You can stay focused on reaching your more important goals while enjoying life more.

- *Enjoy a sense of flow when facing life's more difficult challenges.* Centered stability allows us to meet great challenges with calm and perspective.

Without a strong center, people feel that they are living their lives passively, dominated by external events and forces. Getting centered puts them back in control. What a wonderful and freeing experience it can be.

6

Freedom Follows
Hard Work and Perseverance

*W*hat a difference honest, hard work can make in our lives!
Yet today, we have forgotten that we can achieve more by
trying harder. Perhaps it is because life offers so many vast
rewards that do not seem to demand hard striving. In our newspapers, we read about entrepreneurs who have earned millions of
dollars simply by making deals with other entrepreneurs. We
hear tales of authors and celebrities who gain instant wealth
before they have written a single word or have sung a single
note. We marvel at stories on the evening news about apparently ordinary people who earn instant fortunes by simply buying
lottery tickets.

The message that *easier is better* seems to have gained a hold
over our minds. Yet is it true? Is easier really better? No, it is not.
Even today, we cannot achieve our greatest potential in life without engaging in hard and difficult labors.

The psychologist Abraham Maslow was a student of human
behavior. Yet unlike most other behavioral scientists, he did not
dwell on what was wrong with human beings or what they
couldn't do. Instead, he devoted his life to the study of what was
right about human beings and what they could accomplish. He
was a scientist of human potential.

A famous story about Maslow relates that, late in his life, he
suffered a heart attack. Shortly afterward, he was reported to have
made a statement that, though cited in different ways by different people, surely merits our thoughtfulness.

His statement went something like this:

If you set out to be less than you are capable of being, you will be deeply unhappy for the rest of your life.

That statement resonates with me. When we sell ourselves short, we betray the best that is in us and we will be deeply unhappy for all of our days.

Yet I see people doing just that in our society today, again and again. They are members of what I would call the "walking wounded":

- They are broken of spirit and do not fully remain in life.

- They have given up trying to attain their full growth and stature.

- They lose sight of who they really are and seek their self-definitions in other people.

- They blame the world and all around them instead of accepting responsibility for what is lacking in their own lives.

When I ask such people why they have given up on life in this way, they usually offer about the same explanation. Some say, "Well, I was afraid of failure." Others say, "I have always been afraid that I don't have what it takes." Still other people say, "Becoming what I was supposed to be involved too much hard work and sacrifice."

By giving up, these people betray the best that is in them and become terribly unhappy.

Where can we find wisdom on this sad phenomenon? What can we do?

We can learn to accept responsibility for our own tremendous potential and put it to use.

In his 1994 inaugural speech as president of South Africa, Nelson Mandela offered these words to summarize his vision for his nation:

Our deepest fear is not that we are inadequate. Our deepest fear is that we are powerful beyond measure. For it is our light and not our darkness that frightens us the most.

Nelson Mandela, a man whose wisdom was forged in the furnace of adversity, attained real insight through his years of suffering. When he talks, we need to listen. If he is right in what he has told us just above, it means we are not afraid to act because we fear we'll fail but rather because we fear we will succeed. That is the reason we shy away from the knowledge that we contain something wonderful, grand, and magnificent. We live in fear of having to come to terms with that.

We can stop casting ourselves in the role of victim and begin to act.

Victimization impedes our progress in reaching our dreams. People who suffer from this problem view themselves as perennial scapegoats. They say, "Look what they did to me. Poor me."

George Bernard Shaw, the English playwright, said something extraordinary on this topic in his 1893 book, *Mrs. Warren's Profession.* When I first encountered this statement years ago, I argued with it. Today I no longer question it because I've seen enough of life to know it is absolutely true:

People are always blaming their circumstances for what they are. I don't believe in circumstance. The people who get on in this world are the people who get up and look for the circumstances they want. And if they can't find them, they make them.

Those words tell us to never, ever say that we are victimized by anything or anybody. Because when we say we are victims, we do three things. First, we diminish ourselves. Second, we give away our power. Third, we relinquish our freedom to act to make a difference in our lives and in the world.

One night not long ago, I was at home working on a sermon. I took a break to eat supper, and, as I often do when I'm eating alone, I turned on the television and started flipping through the channels. When I got to the Biography Channel, I saw that Harry Smith, who has spoken at Marble Collegiate Church in the past, was interviewing Barbara Walters. I sat there riveted to that program for the next 90 minutes.

Now I'd invite you to survey all the people in this country and ask them, "Who is the greatest interviewer in America? Who does the best job?" I believe the majority would name Barbara Walters, hands down.

But as I watched that interview and its clips from Barbara Walters' career, I learned that her success was not handed to her. She worked long and hard to achieve it.

Back in the 1960s, she was accepting all kinds of unimportant assignments on television. Finally, due to her ability, she earned the privilege of doing some televised interviews, but even then, she was allowed to interview only women. The task of interviewing important men went only to male broadcasters.

Finally, she started working with Hugh Downs, whom she described as a wonderful, well-centered man with a very healthy ego. The two of them collaborated every morning for many years on the *Today Show*, and they got along beautifully. Barbara continued to grow and grow, honing her craft. Yet she continued to be overlooked as a woman in a man's world.

Finally, ABC invited her to jump to their network, offering her a chance to coanchor ABC's evening news. She took the job partly because no other female newscaster had been given that opportunity before. She was teamed up with Harry Reasoner. According to Barbara Walters, Harry Reasoner did not like her at all. The show I watched presented numerous clips in which he was openly rude to her on the air.

Behind the scenes, things were apparently even worse. Ratings plummeted. Walters went through the most difficult year of her life. Yet later, she was able to look back and say that year was actually the most *important* one of her life. Faced with adversity, she learned, she grew, and she developed character. She became stronger and gained a deep resolve to succeed. She worked hard, and then she worked harder still.

In the interview I watched, Barbara Walters never once said that she had been victimized. She didn't diminish herself that way or give away her power. That attitude was the secret to why she grew stronger and stronger. She did not hide from the power that was within her. She sought to create her own circumstances for success.

We can also look to this marvelous passage from Isaiah, which takes us to another level of insight about the power of refusing to accept the victim role:

> *Those who wait upon the Lord, those who include God, those who allow God to be part of their life journey and process, they shall mount up with wings as the eagle.*

What imagery!

Having faith in yourself is extraordinarily important. But faith in God is even more important. We are never alone. There is a presence that is available to us, and with us, all the time. Even though we may *feel* alone, God remains involved in our lives. That's God's whole purpose for being. As someone once remarked:

> *One with God is a majority.*

When I trust God and don't worry about anything that way, God has a way of coming in and doing exactly what I need. God is always present.

We can commit ourselves to progress, which is an indicator of how hard we have worked and how far we have progressed.

How many of us are really living? How many of us are *fully alive*? Those questions are difficult, but I can suggest one effective way to answer them:

If you're making progress in your life, then you are working and you are really alive.

Think for a moment about the biggest problem you are facing today. Then try to recall the biggest problem you were facing one year ago at this time. If both problems are the same, you are probably not making enough headway. And that means you are not living life fully.

We often don't like to evaluate how much progress we are making. It's uncomfortable. It is much easier to point a finger at someone else and say, "That person over there, he's not growing. He's not moving ahead with life the way I am!" So we see that we are true experts at discerning other people's shortcomings. I know that I am very, very good at it.

I recall one time in my life when I was made especially aware of my own shortcomings.

I had gone to visit the Grand Canyon with my family. One day, we decided to visit a famous sight, Havasee Falls.

If you've been there, you surely remember it. In the midst of an arid area, there's a magnificent waterfall that gushes down at least 300 feet, making everything around it lush and green. Over the centuries, the cascading water has created many natural pools. In the center is one very large pool that is ideal for swimming. At the time we visited, someone had tied a swinging rope to a branch that hung over the water. If you were brave enough, you could grasp that rope, swing out, and plunge into the wonderful cool water.

I have pictures of what happened there on that day. One shows my older son in free fall, arms and legs at every angle, just moments after he let go of the rope. Another shows my younger son with a joyful grin on his face, just as he is falling into the water.

And then there is the picture of me crouching by the tree, holding fast to the rope, filled with crippling fears. What if I broke an ankle? What if I hurt my back?

I just crouched there. I didn't swing out or jump. I let my fears get the best of me and deprive me of that joyful experience. I was too afraid to take a risk and experience something new and wonderful.

What am I saying? I am saying that it is very difficult to turn that corner and get going on the changes we must make in our lives. Yet we also know that people really do change if they commit themselves to the work that is needed to bring about change. Miracles do happen in people's lives. How does it happen? It happens through hard work, and work finally leads to freedom—a heady feeling of freedom over our lives.

We can cultivate an eagerness to create a better future.

Saint Paul, we know, had a brilliant mind. If they had had IQ tests in his day, I believe that his would have gone off the charts. We're very fortunate to have so many of his letters, which record so much of his wisdom. Through them, we come to understand how he overcame problems in his life, and how he got to achieve his power and strength.

Let me paraphrase something Paul wrote in his letter to the Philippians:

> *This one thing I do. I forget what lies in the past and I stretch and strain forward to what lies ahead. I press on toward the goal.*

What was Paul saying? He was saying, in essence, "I have found something that works. I turn my back on the past, which can drag me down and prevent me from moving ahead. I stretch and strain toward the future." Notice too that Paul talked about the *effort* of stretching forward ("I press on . . ."). He wanted to tell people that progress is difficult. It takes work. You have to persevere.

We can strive toward rewards that are not of this world.

Some of you might know Dr. Harry Moody's name. In his extraordinary book *The Five Stages of the Soul* (Doubleday, 1998), he writes that when he was a young man, he spent time at a

Roman Catholic retreat center in northern California. It was a curious thing for him to do because he had been brought up a strict Lutheran. It was like entering into a new world for him.

On the second day at the retreat, he met a nun named Sister Anne Marie. She was in her late sixties. He told her that he felt he was on a journey with his life. She replied that she, too, had been actively searching for something since childhood.

She said, "When I was a little girl, I searched for the affection and the approval of my parents. Then when I got to school, I searched for good grades so I would be liked by everybody. When I grew up, I searched for a husband and a career. I got married. I couldn't have children, so I searched for a way to adopt a child."

Then she said, "I came into this nunnery when I was 34 years old, after my husband and son had been killed in a boating accident. After that tragedy, I devoted my life to prayer and good works. I'm now 68 years old and I'm still on a search."

Harry Moody said it was very helpful to him, as a young man, to hear an older person, far along on her journey, say she had never stopped searching and pressing forward.

And then she said these words, which made a deep impression on him:

> As I got older, I stopped looking for answers in the material world because the material world contains only things that will pass from sight. The difference in my life began when I began to search for that one permanent thing in the universe—when I began my search for God.

She was telling the young man to keep seeking. She was saying that if he would keep pressing ahead, there was a spiritual guarantee that the answer he was seeking would come.

We can learn to persevere despite setbacks.

Over the years, I have learned one more great secret about perseverance, about pressing on with the search. As you keep searching for answers, it is essential to keep on *expecting* that they will come to you. Expect something wonderful to happen. Expect tomorrow to be better than today. Expect that your problem will be solved. Expect that you will find comfort if you are troubled. Expect, expect, and then expect some more.

I have seen it time and again. Expectation makes great things much more likely to happen. My friend Richard Lewis recently sent this story that serves as a wonderful parable to illustrate just that point. It seems that a woman who had been ill went to see her doctor. He told her she had only about 3 months to live and that she should get her affairs in order. So she got her material and financial decisions made, and then she called her minister.

"I'd like to plan my funeral with you," she said. She then told him about the Scriptures she wanted read, the hymns that she wanted sung, and the dress she wanted to be buried in. She also said she wanted to be buried with her favorite Bible. The minister agreed to all these things.

But then she said, "I have one more request. I'd like to be buried with a fork in my right hand."

And the minister said, "A fork in your right hand? What is that about?"

And she said, "In my long life, I attended many dinners at church. Every time people were cleaning the table, they would say, 'Keep your fork.' So I always knew that keeping a fork meant that something better was about to happen. I was always rewarded with chocolate pie or deep-dish apple pie."

"But," she said to the minister, "I don't want you to tell anybody why I have a fork until you give my funeral sermon."

The day of her funeral finally did come. She was laid out in her favorite dress, holding her favorite Bible, with a fork in her right hand. And people were buzzing around and asking, "What is that all about? What is that all about?"

In his sermon, the minister told the story about how she knew that the best was yet to come and that holding a fork had become her personal symbol for that idea. The minister told the congregation that he, too, wanted to be buried holding a fork. It was a matter of faith.

Without that kind of clear vision of what the future can hold, we lose our willingness to keep moving forward.

Finally, we can cultivate an honest enjoyment of hard work and its well-earned rewards.

How much our relationship to work has changed over the last century! Only a few generations ago, our grandfathers were likely to be laborers or tradesmen. Our grandmothers engaged in a range of hard, exhausting labor that might include raising children. Overall, people were involved in the kind of exhausting, self-testing work that led them to a better understanding of both themselves and the world.

As I mentioned at the beginning of this chapter, we seem to have lost sight of the value of hard, exhausting work. Depending on the nature of that work, its reward might be:

- A keener knowledge of one's own intelligence, strength, and abilities.

- An intimate knowledge of some real part of the world— the process of parenting, perhaps, or of cutting wood or farming a field.

- Respect that is earned from the people around us. I believe that even today, hard work can earn us legitimate respect as leaders.

Today, we often seem to have lost our access to these simple benefits of hard work. Yet the remedy is both simple and immediate. It is simple hard work, often invested with the kind of passion we explored earlier in this book.

Deepening Our Understanding

Hard work can act as a freeing force in our lives, empowering us to achieve more. Its benefits are immediately apparent:

- We come to be seen as leaders—exceptional individuals who serve as examples to others.

- By working hard and with dedication, we arrive at our full potential as human beings.

- We gain the kind of keen insight into ourselves, and into the world, that comes with experience.

In the end, we accept more responsibility for what is taking place in our lives, and we have a more profound level of control over our destiny. All through simple hard work and its remarkable power to lift and broaden the experience of living in this world.

7

Freedom Follows
Being Present in the Moment

*E*arlier we explored the harm we do to ourselves when we cannot establish a healthy relationship with the past. In this chapter, we will look at our relationship with the future:

Are we living in the moment, at being present and involved in what is taking place in our lives right now? Or are we always concerned about tomorrow?

Most of us go through our lives distracted, preoccupied, and unable to focus on the present. Often we succumb to worry about what will happen, or might happen, in our lives. Tomorrow becomes more real, and more pressing, than today. When we allow that to happen, we lose our ability to deal effectively with what is happening in the present. It is not, however, inevitable that we lose sight of the present. The following strategies—which are reassuring and often quite simple to use—can help us get our lives back in focus quickly.

Not long ago, a member of Marble Collegiate Church approached me with a question. He had noticed that the following Sunday's sermon was going to be about living in the present. He said, "Arthur, do you mind if I send something to you?" and I said, "Please do."

He sent me a poem by an anonymous writer. It clearly describes the life of a person who lives entirely in anticipation of the days to come:

First I was dying to finish high school and start college.
And then I was dying to finish college and start working.
And then I was dying to marry and to have children.
And then I was dying for my children to grow old
enough for school so I could return to work.
And then I was dying to retire.
And now, I am dying . . . and suddenly I realize that I
forgot to live.

Now, those words might not constitute great literature. But they unquestionably describe a problem that afflicts many of us. We have trouble focusing on the now.

Great thinkers have also recognized the necessity of living in the present. Rainer Maria Rilke, a poet with a brilliant and insightful mind, once observed that our lives are not effective because we enter the present moment "unfinished, unable, and distracted."

We also know that Ralph Waldo Emerson, one of the greatest thinkers America has ever produced, wrote these words in his 1841 essay, *Self-Reliance*. They remind us about the necessity of giving up the illusion that we can influence tomorrow by worrying about it today:

Finish each day and be done with it. You have done what
you could; some blunders and absurdities have crept in;
forget them as soon as you can. Tomorrow is a new day; you
shall begin it serenely and with too high a spirit to be
encumbered with your old nonsense.

Those statements summarize so well what happens when we direct all of our focus toward future events over which we exert no control:

- *We live a "shadow" existence.* We speed right past the joys that life holds for us, never able to fully perceive or grasp them. Love, the joy of children, and the experience of daily life all fade away, dull and secondary.

- *Our effectiveness is impaired.* You have doubtless spent time in the company of underachieving people who are distracted and unable to focus on what must be done today. I believe that many of them have become that way because of excessive worry about events they cannot control in the future. Without appropriate focus on the present, they are greatly crippling their effectiveness in the world.

- *Anxiety surges to the breaking point.* We can only control the *now*. Believing that we can control the future completely fosters only unrealistic expectations and acute worry and stress.

If you have fallen victim to these problems, how can you turn your life around and live more in today?

We can open our senses in the present.

We can all pause to look around us and be overwhelmed by the sights, smells, and tastes that flow into us from the outside world.

Simply *notice*. See the sky. Breathe the air. Feel the world all around. The practice of finding stillness, we know, can be a great help in this process. We also know that Ralph Waldo Emerson and Henry David Thoreau and their fellow American transcendentalist philosophers made a practice of spending time in the outdoors. They placed great stock in solitude and nature, and their beliefs are worth incorporating into our modern lives. Without a sensory awareness of each day, after all, we lose sight of a wondrous present that is ever so much more beautiful than the past or the future could ever be.

A few years ago, my wife and I shared an experience that highlighted just that lesson very effectively. We had the opportunity to go on a safari in Africa. It was one of our most memorable and unique trips. There were only seven people in our group, and among them was a couple from California. The husband in that pair was what you might call a shutter nut. It seemed that he took a picture of something every 10 seconds. He was always clicking, clicking, clicking.

I recall that one morning we were to take a ride on horseback along the plains of Kenya. As you may know, you can get right up alongside giraffes, elephants, wildebeests, and other animals when you are riding on horseback. We were all excited about the experience we were about to share. Yet our photographer was concerned with something else. He started that morning by shouting at his wife, "Honey! Honey! The batteries have fallen out of my camera!" Then he shouted again, "Honey, Honey, the batteries are gone! I can't take any pictures!"

In a very calm voice, his wife replied, "Now you can enjoy the scenery." And so could we.

How often are we like that man, so preoccupied with secondary experiences-to-be that we miss the most beautiful things in life? It seems that we live in such a state of anticipation that we never actually enjoy the moment when it arrives.

Yet we can look around ourselves, wherever we are. This is a gorgeous moment! Take a moment to sense and feel all that is around you. I hope that you are warm and comfortable. Maybe you are wearing some favorite item of clothing. Perhaps you are in a place where the light is beautiful or your surroundings are beloved and dear. Perhaps you are listening to wonderful music, or smelling flowers, or watching your cat lie in a patch of sunshine on the floor. Perhaps you feel energy, faith, and love. How wonderful life is! Live in the moment and breathe it in. It is far more real than tomorrow could ever be.

We can actively share the journey with the people around us.

Love the people who share your journey, moment by moment and hour by hour. Remember, life is *now*, and as much as we might want our human relationships to go on forever, that would be impossible. We need to grasp them joyfully, before time changes them or takes them away.

There are some very practical ways to make this happen. Starting today, we can make it a point to:

- *Simply take more time with the people we love and cherish.* That sounds like simple advice. But more often than not, we are so involved in rushing from place to place that we neglect to pause to enjoy a quiet time or a good conversation with the people who mean the most to us.

- *Increase your power to notice.* Pay attention to what that spouse or important person is wearing today. Ask about what will take place during his or her day, and, at the end of the day, ask about what happened. The simple act of noticing anchors us in the present joy of going through life in the company of the people we love.

- *Really listen to what the people you love are saying.* Instead of rushing on to the next moment or the next thought, strive to *empathize* and feel the emotions behind their words.

- *Practice some rituals that enrich your relationships.* Anniversaries and father's and mother's day are important, but not enough. Make it a habit to actively remember together important milestones from past experiences with beloved people. Say, "I'm thinking about Christmas last year, how much fun we had," or "Let's take out those photos from our honeymoon and enjoy it all over again."

Simple, joyful practices can bring us into a deeper appreciation of the value of the present.

We can focus on the purpose for the life that we are living today.

One way to become more grounded in the present is to simply ask, "Why am I here today?" and then to listen to the ideas your mind formulates in answer.

If that process is not productive (and it might not be because you are attacking a major life question in a very direct way), you can try introducing it more gently into your thinking. I can suggest a way to begin. We each have a continuous, internal conversation with ourselves in which we ask basic questions:

- "Where am I going to spend today?"

- "What is my top priority or goal for today?"

- "What will I wear?"

- "What will I prepare for dinner?"

With only a little effort, we can bring this internal dialogue to higher and higher levels so that we get beyond mundane issues and encounter what we might call our "higher selves."

After you have started your day and answered all the smaller questions about your clothing and your schedule and your breakfast, try to feed the bigger ones right into the same stream. As you walk from your home in the morning or take a break at work, ask, "What is my purpose?" and "What is it that I have been put on this earth to do?"

By inaugurating these bigger questions into our internal dialog in this way, we gently orient ourselves toward higher things that are always operating in the present moment. When we don't fully expect it, answers appear. We hear remarkable answers, like these:

- "I am here to be kind to people."

- "I am here to bring joy to children."

- "I am here to alleviate pain."

Not all such answers will be "the" answer to why you are here today, spending your life in this glorious world. Some will be worth developing, and others not. Yet they all can become part of a process you are working on as you seek a path that leads to a fuller realization of why you have been put on this earth.

I will share a secret with you about this process. Over time, it becomes closer and closer to praying. In fact, we could even call this interior dialogue "conversational prayer." I would urge you to give it a try.

We can stop predicting and worrying.

Worrying keeps us continually, and negatively, mired in an unhealthy focus about the future.

In his book *Good Stress, Bad Stress* (Marlowe & Company, 2002), my coauthor and friend Barry Lenson sums up the problem this way:

> *You're caught in a chain of scenarios for events which will probably never happen. The lure of the pattern is the unspoken belief that, through worrying, you will be able to control the outcome of what is about to happen to you. You think you are planning, but in reality you are obsessing. Even when we realize this is the case, we are often unable to break free of the pattern's hold.*

There are many ways to chase away the illusion that worry will help us prepare for tomorrow. We can pause to recall past events that we were fearing—an exercise that often shows that the negative consequences we obsess about rarely come to pass. Another effective approach is to conduct a worst-case-scenario exercise in which we write down the worst thing that might result from something we are anguishing about today. This exercise shows us that even the worst things we expect rarely have the power to completely derail or harm us. If you learn tomorrow that a grating sound you heard from under your car today will require a costly repair, you will find a way to cope with it. If your mortgage application gets turned down, you can apply at another bank. We are all more resilient than we believe, and we encounter that inner strength in the present, not an imaginary future.

We can invest each day with spiritual meaning.

Of the many words and Scriptures we read as part of the services at my church, one of the most beloved is also the simplest:

> *This is the day that the Lord has made. Let us be glad and rejoice in it!*

Notice the supreme power in that plainness.

Today, not tomorrow, is the day the Lord has made. Tomorrow does not exist. Today is the opportunity we have before us.

And how are we to make the best use of this supreme gift, this present day? God does not tell us to worry. God does not tell us to plan, or to make a to-do list and set priorities, or to focus on our goals. God simply tells us to rejoice and be glad today. If we do that, we have begun to control our lives.

How often we lose sight of the effective power of simply living with joy, in the present. It is a practical power as well as a spiritual one.

One day, a woman in our church called me to say that she was going for a job interview the next day. Would I pray for her success, she wanted to know? Of course I would. As we spoke, I was impressed because she didn't sound at all nervous or apprehensive about the interview. She seemed calm and serene.

I commented on this, and she told me her secret for meeting difficult or challenging situations. "I always pray God into the room ahead of me. I ask God to provide an atmosphere that will be conducive to a good meeting. And," she said, "God has never let me down."

I am confident that, no matter what your religion or beliefs may be, you can do something similar. You can sanctify the place where something difficult will take place, inviting some higher presence in. It is a sure way to become courageous in the face of troubles or opposition.

The Book of Joshua tells us that after the death of Moses, the responsibility for leading the Israelites into the Promised Land passed to Joshua. Joshua, the Israelites' new leader, was called upon to shoulder a daunting set of responsibilities. And I would assume he was very worried about how well he would handle them. Yet God said to him, "As I was with Moses, so I will be with you. I will not fail you or forsake you. . . . Only be strong and very courageous, being careful to act in accordance with all the laws that my servant Moses commanded you." And God finishes these instructions with beautiful words:

> *I hereby command you: Be strong and courageous; do not be frightened or dismayed, for the Lord your God is with you wherever you go.*

God is truly with us, wherever we go. We are never alone. Where do we sense God's presence? Where is the place where he lends his help to us? It is surely not tomorrow, but today—the opportunity-filled day that "the Lord has made."

Deepening Our Understanding

In this chapter, we have explored a rich array of personal and spiritual tools we can use to bring today into sharp, productive focus. When we do this, we receive many rich returns:

- *We experience more joy in living.* The joys of today are always greater than the anticipated pleasures of tomorrow. And the worries about tomorrow can, and should, fade away.

- *We become more effective.* Today is like the fulcrum of a powerful lever we can use to control tomorrow. We cannot let it go. Worrying will not build a better future; rather, a better future will be built by the big and small actions we take today with a clear mind that is anchored in the present.

- *We feel calmer and more in control of our lives.* We cannot ever fully control the future, but we can experience the sense of control that results from an ability to make good choices and live joyously in the present hour.

Freedom can never be found tomorrow. It is ever in the moment—something we can grasp only today.

8

Freedom Follows
Discipline and Priorities

*A*s you strive to regain freedom in your life, I hope you will put "growth in self-discipline" and "set my life priorities" at the very top of your list. I also hope you are willing to devote time to the process. Like all things that offer major life benefits, getting your priorities in place doesn't come easily. It involves frustration and trial and error. Sometimes, it can even involve recovering from failure. But down deep, we know that we need to keep at it because it's the process that ultimately brings us to fullness and effectiveness in our lives. In the end, a focused and disciplined life becomes a freer life.

Early in my ministry, I was most fortunate to enjoy very close associations with several men of faith who were also men of very, very high achievement. Several of them had achieved worldwide influence. They were a credit to themselves, to their families, to their communities, and even to the nation.

I was awed by them and I was curious. I was anxious to know how they did what they did. What were the secrets to their success?

Through the years, I've often talked and written about two of these men, Homer Surbeck and Amos Parrish. I've tried to absorb their lessons, and I've told their stories because they shaped my story and shaped my life. I'd like to include their stories for you here in the hope that they will have the same influence on you, to encourage you to shape or reshape something important about your life.

Homer Surbeck, born in 1901, would be more than 100 years old, if he were alive today. He died about 5 years ago, at the age of 95. When I came to my church 34 years ago, he was a managing partner in one of the largest and most prestigious law firms in the United States. He was an extraordinary human being. Over the years, knowledgeable people have told me that when Homer Surbeck was in the prime of his career, he was regarded as the finest litigator in the country. Nobody could reach him, he was so good. Several people have even told me that if Homer Surbeck had represented Bell Telephone, it never would have been broken up. He was that good.

Homer was as honest as the sunshine is bright. He was what people sometimes call "a straight arrow," one of the few people I have known who lived by, and trusted, the Golden Rule. In his speeches and comments, he would often say, "Do unto others . . . It works! It works!"

When we were having lunch one day, I finally got the courage to ask a question that had been on my mind: "Homer, what do you think is the key to success?"

His answer came in a flash. He didn't have to think, contemplate, or ponder. Before either one of us could blink an eye, he said: "Arthur, the key to success is self-discipline."

I knew at once that he was right. But I have to admit that I didn't like the answer. I didn't like it because I knew that self-discipline requires hard work. It demands the resolve to keep going despite all of life's frustrations, failures, and disappointments. At that time, I was confused in my own life. I was trying to get a handle on so many challenges, trying to get focused and organized, trying to get disciplined. But I could see clearly that Homer had given me the secret I needed to hear.

Later on, I learned why Homer Surbeck had that answer right on the tip of his tongue. He'd been born in Rapid City, South Dakota, the child of educated people. His father was a Presbyterian preacher in that town. When Homer was in first grade, his teacher came to visit. She brought bad news, news that brought tears to Homer's parents' eyes: "Your son is not very bright. He never will be a good student."

Homer would not be very successful at life, she told them. They had better get used to the idea.

Yet his parents did not take that news lying down. They got involved in helping him learn. As he was learning to read, they taught him how to pinpoint the most important idea in any paragraph, page, and chapter. They encouraged him to memorize that idea first, before worrying about anything else. If he could get that most important point in line, they taught him, everything else would fall into place.

It took that young child a few years to get the handle on concepts like that. But when he had grasped a number of them, astonishingly, he rose to the top of his class. He was top in his high school graduating class. He went to college at the South Dakota School of Mines. Then he got accepted at Yale Law School, one of the most prestigious law schools in the world. And when Homer Surbeck graduated from Yale Law School, he was again number 1 in his class.

Amos Parrish was another mentor in the early days of my career. One day, when I was singing the praises of Homer Surbeck to Amos Parrish, I said, "Amos, he must have a very high IQ. It must be off the charts."

Amos said, "No, Arthur, you're wrong. I've watched Homer Surbeck for years. He has average intelligence. Many of the successful people you know have a higher IQ. But he is the most disciplined man I have ever met."

Amos Parrish was speaking of the beauty, the power, and the effectiveness of the disciplined mind.

I have known many, many very capable people who never realized their full potential because they lacked discipline. They are like diamonds that have never been polished or cut into neat, bright facets by a skilled jeweler. Their brightness remains trapped within, unable to emerge into the light of day.

When we allow ourselves to drift off course in that way, we experience a life of unfulfilled possibilities and frustration:

- *We lose our dreams and grand plans, never to find them again.* When we are young people, we are ready to take on the world! We look ahead and can envision ourselves accomplishing grand things in our lives. Yet unless we apply hard work to put those plans in order, those visions remain unformed, never to emerge.

- *We live our lives at the whim and will of other people.* Through organization, we become followers of our own plans, not those of others, and we emerge as leaders. After all, what is a leader but someone who has applied the discipline to see his or her dreams become reality in the world?

- *We put our dreams on hold and risk becoming embittered.* I recall one woman I knew who spoke for years about a novel she planned to complete "one day." When she died, her most important life project had come to little more than a notebook full of scribbling. Just a little discipline applied over the years would have resulted in a completed work—perhaps not a masterpiece, but at the very least, a permanent record of that woman's creative mind.

And when can we begin the process of achieving a disciplined mind and life?

The first step is for us to really think about what is important in our lives.

In other words, we can carefully define our priorities. I am not referring to our daily priorities—the errands to run and the phone calls to make. I am talking instead about long-range goals that we can, and should, establish for the most important missions we would like to fulfill in our lives.

Our personal missions are sometimes clear to us, crystallized out of our experiences, education, training, and abilities. If you are a physician, for example, it may occur to you one day that your purpose in life is to alleviate pain. If you are a teacher, you may already know that your life purpose is to impart a love of learning that will gratify all your students for the entire course of their lives.

At other times, a personal mission can be harder to discern. In countless small, spiritual ways, it appears and surrounds us until we finally realize that it has already been present, working within us. I recall that many years ago I had a dream that gave me a sudden glimpse of what my mission would be in the years ahead. I dreamt of an impressive chain that was made up of massive links. Later I saw that the dream was a message for me in my life work. I came to a strong church that had impressive links in its past; I am referring to a long line of remarkable leaders. Through my dream, I saw that I was to be another link, someone who took a place between the church's ministers of the past and those of its future. I see this mission in very practical ways. Even in meetings and while conducting practical, day-to-day affairs, I am often aware that I am acting as a link between the past and the future.

Isn't it true that, most of the time, we allow life to establish our priorities for us? We deal with what is seemingly urgent, things that are often not important. Instead, we need to think about what is really important in our lives. That often means being open to life's messages and clues.

Next, we can be ready to try, and then try again.

Making profound change is always difficult. I recently heard that, on average, it takes 19 tries for the average person to give up smoking. Nineteen tries! That shows a remarkable amount of determination. But if you can make those 19 tries and if you can succeed, you're stronger, you're organized, and much harder to defeat.

Whatever the next problem that lies in your path, you know you can overcome it because self-discipline has done its work. You're free.

But such freedom doesn't come on a silver platter. It is the result of discipline, hard work, effort, and doing your emotional and spiritual homework.

As a preacher, I know that self-discipline doesn't come easily. For example, it takes an enormous amount of time to prepare a sermon. I write a section. Then I write it again. Then again. Often, I go back to the beginning and rethink my fundamental concept. Finally, after repeated tries, I begin to sense that I have gained a foothold and am moving forward with some positive momentum toward my goal.

Repeated, frustrated efforts are often needed if we are to get discipline working on our side.

As the Old Testament tells us in Proverbs:

Keep straight the path of your feet and all your ways will be sure. Do not swerve to the right or to the left. Turn your feet away from evil.

I believe these words are telling us not to allow ourselves to be swayed from keeping on the good, higher path. Because no matter how disciplined we *think* we are in our approach to certain challenges, life surprises us.

We can be ready to make sacrifices to reach our goals.

On occasion my wife will say, "Arthur, can we go out on Saturday night for dinner?"

Most often I say, "No, Lea, I can't do that."

"Why not?"

"Because I have a sermon to give on Sunday."

Lea understands. She has seen that the more work time I spend, the more concentrated effort, the more struggle, the more reading, the more prayer, the more absorption, the more going over and over the material, the more freedom I have.

To arrive at that great feeling, I know I need the discipline, the effort, the pain that goes into it. It requires tremendous self-discipline, but the rewards are great. Learning this was one of the greatest things I ever did.

We can put the power of time on our side.

We live in a world where faster is often confused with better. As we build our priorities and plans, it is important to remember that slow life processes can often be preferable to quick ones.

I have a friend who rents an apartment in an old brownstone building here in New York City. It is in one of three wonderful buildings that are owned by one man. One day, my friend asked his landlord how he had managed to buy three such wonderful buildings. Did he have money from his family that let him get started? My friend was amazed by his landlord's answer. "I worked in a store for 15 years before I bought my first building," he said. "I knew that if I set aside a certain amount from my salary every week, I could afford to buy a building in 15 years, so I made a plan to do that. Following my plan meant living very modestly, but I stuck to it and I did it."

This is the same principle that my friend Dr. Kenneth Ruge applied to writing his first book, *Where Do I Go from Here?* (McGraw-Hill, 1998). He made a master plan and wrote just a little bit every day until it was done: a process he calls "eating an elephant." "How do you eat an elephant?" he explains. "One bite at a time."

So as you plan your life's goals and priorities, remember that time can be added to your plan. It is an essential element of discipline that we overlook too often today—and it can make the difference between a plan that works and one that doesn't.

We are our own source of greatest help.

It is fine to rely on a group of other people to support us and help us reach our goals. In my own church, surely, I would never be able to handle all the details and get everything done without the assistance of so many skilled, wonderful, and committed individuals.

Yet when it comes to keeping my life disciplined, the task is up to me. Only I can keep my time and my life on track, no one else can do it for me. If I lose sight of what I want to accomplish, no one will ever remind me.

Sam Levenson, the American humorist, wrote in his best-selling book *Everything But Money* (Simon & Schuster, 1963) that one of his father's favorite sayings was this:

> *If you need a helping hand, you'll find it at the end of your sleeve.*

That is fine advice for us all to heed. Striving toward our life goals is a process that is, in the end, something we cannot delegate. It is entirely up to us.

We can seek spiritual support in the process of building discipline.

I think it is revealing to note that the words *discipline* and *disciple* share the same Latin root. I believe the message is that we can become stronger, and achieve more through discipline, when we enter into a new relationship with God.

When we, like Homer Surbeck and Amos Parrish, become disciplined in our religious practice, we can achieve more in the real world. Whatever your faith may be, forge a deeper alliance with it and you will be surprised to see how it will increase your effectiveness and level of achievement in the real world.

Deepening Our Understanding

In an interview published in *Life* magazine, Robert Frost was quoted as saying, "Life is tons of discipline." And he was right. Once we put the power of discipline to work for us, our lives are transformed:

- *We accomplish a great deal in our lives.* Now, that is an obvious benefit of discipline, to be sure. But it is worth noting all the same. When we look at Beethoven, we see that he wrote nine symphonies. Maya Angelou wrote *I Know Why the Caged Bird Sings* and many other wondrous works. Michelangelo painted the ceiling of the Sistine Chapel. We can marvel at how individuals can attain so much when they have had but one life to live. The answer is simple. They had *discipline.*

- *We become unique.* Each life is unique, unlike any other. Only through discipline can we move in the direction that is right for us and create a life of achievements that is uniquely and entirely our own.

And, of course, we become free. Discipline, which appears to be a weight upon us, is really a weight lifted off our shoulders. It is the one sure tool we have to take our lives wherever we want to.

9

Freedom Follows a Healthy Relationship with Money

---

*T*here is a nearly universal belief that wealth brings freedom. Yet in my experience, many people are unable to keep that truth in perspective and realize that money and freedom, while related, are really two different things.

Of course, money is important. Without it, you can do very little. It is necessary for food, shelter, and clothing. Money not only provides sustenance, it enables choice and independence. Yet we also know that money, and the fixation with it, can actually take over some people's lives and make them *less* free.

I recently heard an interview on National Public Radio with Charles Barkley, the outstanding NBA basketball player who has just retired. Barkley, who has recently written a new book called *I May Be Wrong, But I Doubt It* (Random House, 2002), turns out to be a very thoughtful man. As I listened, I was not too surprised that many of his thoughts centered on issues of establishing a healthy relationship with money. After all, many athletes earn extraordinarily high salaries.

As Barkley rose to star status in sports, he was suddenly very wealthy. It is a problem faced, he says, by many young athletes who are suddenly given immense sums of money when they sign with professional sports teams. Like many of them, Barkley immediately bought cars and moved to a fancy new home. Like them, he began traveling with an "entourage" of people, paying the bill to put them up in hotels.

And like many of them, he used his money to maintain his relationships with people he knew while he was growing up. I recall that he told the interviewer that when he couldn't be there with his old friends, he would send them money instead. Yet he soon learned that money can't be a substitute for friendship. He learned this lesson in a painful way. When he stopped sending money to old friends, they withdrew their friendship from him.

Barkley cited other ills that can be caused when we attempt to substitute money for friendship, love, spirituality, and the many things that are the "real" currency of the human experience.

People who are suddenly wealthy are not alone in running into problems where money is concerned. We can all run into trouble with it, not because of what it is (just a currency of exchange, after all) but because of our attitudes about it. We tend to believe popular myths about wealth. As a result our lives can be misguided. Let's look at some of these myths.

Myth 1: Money and material wealth bring happiness. We live in the most prosperous country in the world. Yet I am not far from the truth in stating that Americans, overall, are not a terribly happy people. Even the wealthiest people among us seem unfulfilled. In fact, some of the wealthiest people I have known have been the most desperately unhappy, the most isolated people—people whose lives were empty.

Myth 2: Most of life's problems can be solved through the application of material wealth. Money will pay the rent, buy a new car, and send our kids to college. It will provide creature comforts and numerous pleasures. It can even impart status to us. But as Barkley underscored so clearly, it can never substitute for love. Money cannot nurture a child, affirm a loved one, or satisfy the human need for intimate relationships. It cannot comfort a grieving soul. As many people who become ill know all too well, it cannot replace lost health. Money, or the promise of it, can in fact act as a distraction, a misguided promise of answers to life's deepest needs. It cannot bring peace or wisdom or courage.

Myth 3: Money and wealth equal prosperity. The dictionary defines *prosperity* as "the condition of being successful or thriving." Yet true prosperity does not require great material wealth. Do you know many wealthy people who are successful or thriving beyond merely financial or worldly standards? Think of people you know who are full of life and joy, who bring goodness to the world, and who grow through each of life's challenges. Is there any real relationship between their financial status and their success at living? I would wager you that there is not. I could name many people who are really prosperous, though not wealthy. They include college professors, merchants, nurses, cab drivers—the list could go on and on. Are some wealthy people prosperous? Of course there are. But being rich does not guarantee that anyone will be truly successful in life's important things, or truly thriving.

So then what is prosperity?

You are prosperous when you feel blessed regardless of what you have, and when you then take that blessing, that abundance, whether large or small, and you share it with other people and with the world.

Again, we need to talk about hard work and earning our freedoms. Achieving real prosperity requires work—work we must do both within our careers and outside of them. The person who is in that flow is elevated to a higher level of the spirit.

How can we achieve real prosperity?

We can trade in spiritual currency.

The idea of "spiritual currency" may strike you as somewhat curious. After all, currency is money, and what does that have to do with living in a higher, spiritual place?

The kind of currency I am referring to is something quite different from money. It is a different kind of currency we can use in all areas of our lives when we open ourselves up to the notion that there is a higher presence in our lives.

For example, when we accept the idea that peace is within us, not somewhere "out there," we receive a benefit that we can enjoy in many areas of our lives—in our relationships, in our careers, in all areas. That is an example of spiritual currency—a benefit you can "spend" in any area of your life.

We become prosperous—in the sense of being rich in our spiritual lives—when we are spiritually alive and seeking to live in the mysterious, exciting, stretching kingdom of God. The road to this kind of prosperity is both easier and harder than the road to material wealth. It is easier because it is simpler. It is harder because simplicity requires focus, conviction, and discipline. Simplicity requires us to put away distracting complications.

We can exchange blessings as gifts.

Blessing. What a word! What a force it can be in our lives! It is a positive spiritual force that actually increases in power and reserve as we give it away. It is a simple recognition that where we are and what we are doing comes not from us, but from some higher place. When we pass that blessing along to others, we come to live in a higher place.

Consider:

- Blessing is the good.

- Blessing is affirmation.

- Blessing is helpfulness.

- Blessing is the divine embracing the human.

- Blessing is the ultimate feeling of openness and empathy. It is an open-ended offer to be nurturing toward all other people.

Blessing makes everything sacred. It is thousands of times more powerful than money could ever become. There is enormous power in blessing. And it is something we can all do.

At Marble Collegiate Church, we have a wonderful tradition, a long moment of silent prayer that is part of every service. During this quiet time, I ask often that we use this time to bless one another. We bless all the people around us, those in front of us, those behind us, those across the aisle. Every time we do it, the energy level rises. Everyone feels an enormous lift. As we give blessings, everyone feels lifted. We are being blessed by the act of blessing itself.

The concept of blessing is an important part of our religious traditions.

Haven't we all felt the joy of a human touch? Children want, and need, the touch of a loving parent. Adults need it too. There is little as uplifting as a hug or warm embrace. Even a simple handshake can be deeply reassuring and satisfying if it is done with feeling.

We can find the real blessing wealth that resides in this moment.

But there's another dimension to blessing that I commend to you. It is taking an inventory of your blessings. Here is part of my own inventory for today:

> I feel blessed right now to be here, writing in my church. I sense an enormous amount of love and faith in this sacred place. I am blessed by it.
>
> I am blessed by a wonderful wife.
>
> I am blessed by my children.
>
> I am also blessed by stepchildren and grandchildren!
>
> I am blessed because I have food to eat and a roof over my head.

I am blessed by my friendships.

I am blessed by the problems I am facing today because I can work through them.

I am blessed by some pressing challenges I will face in meetings later today. They will keep me humble, and, as I solve them, I will grow. With luck, they might even bring me closer to my own truth and to God as well.

I am blessed by having the joy of blessing others. It is a wonderful force that is available to me at any point during the day. To bless others. To bless you as you read these words. To bless strangers walking by. It is a spiritual currency that is available to us at every moment, and it is packed with power.

What world currency can ever equal this power, the force of blessing? Not the dollar. Not the euro. Not the franc or the peso or the mark, though they be piled up to the sky. Through blessing, we have the potential to arrive at true, fully evolved prosperity—a prosperity that exceeds the worth of dollars and cents. It is the kind of prosperity that supercedes everything that is material.

Some people may say this kind of prosperity is not real or tangible. It is both of those things, and more. People who have mastered this concept, and who live it, feel themselves fulfilled and happy.

We can exchange the currency of sharing.

The next idea is also simple, yet difficult for most of us:

> *Whatever you have, whatever abundance, whether great or small, share it. Find ways of giving it away.*

As you follow this advice, you will experience the truth of the teaching from Ecclesiastes:

As you cast your bread upon the waters, in time it will come back to you.

This is one of God's most exciting laws. And it really works, by enriching the lives of everyone who takes part: the givers and the receivers. As you have no doubt observed, the most prosperous people are those who have found ways to give.

Chapter 11 of Proverbs tells us:

Some give freely, yet grow all the richer. Others withhold what is due, and only suffer want. A generous person will be enriched, and one who gives water will be watered.

This is a lesson I have learned in my own life. There have been times when I have known that I would be in the flow, sharing with others and I held back. At such times, I was always the loser.

Nearly a half century ago, there lived and ministered in New York City a remarkable Episcopal priest named Sam Shoemaker. He was a bigger-than-life human being and a gifted communicator. People who remember Sam Shoemaker's sermons have told me that he often used a colorful metaphor to explain the necessity of giving. He said that when water fills a bucket to overflowing, the excess spills and is wasted. He counseled a better way that went something like this:

Turn that bucket over, kick out the bottom, and make it into a pipeline. Then what you receive flows through you to others and does some good.

This is what prosperity is about. We are prosperous when we respond to blessings by passing them on. We enrich ourselves and enrich the world.

Not long ago, I had a conversation with a young professional woman who seems to have mastered the reality that the more we can give, the more we have. She is a woman approaching age

50. She has no children. Last year, her much-loved mother passed away. She has a career that makes great demands on her time. Some people in her position would be unhappy, despite their wealth. But she was not unhappy. She told me that the greatest thing she does, the thing that enriches her life in countless ways, is giving. She gives some of her scant time to helping children read at a home in New York for battered women and their families. This brings her into contact with children and enriches her life in countless ways. She doesn't have enough time to volunteer at the Metropolitan Museum of Art, but she gives them money each year and relishes the chance to attend previews of shows before they are opened to the general public. She has made many friends through this activity. She also invests real time and energy in her friendships, which fortify her and enhance her life in many ways. She has taken an active role with her god daughter and enjoys the wonderful experiences they share.

I believe she has mastered the practice of a law that could be called the "incredible law of supply." For those who trust this law, and those who yield to it, provision is made for every important life need to be met. And I am not exaggerating.

We have all heard the saying "The Lord will provide." This is exactly what the law of supply is about.

The Lord does provide. I know it from my own experience and from watching other people. People who believe in this law and yield to it discover that it is impossible to give anything away. When you get into the flow of this law, what you give away comes back.

I once heard somebody say that if you give freely, in the right spirit, it is virtually impossible to give a dollar away. When you give a dollar away, with an open heart, not counting the cost or looking for a return, you don't get just a dollar back. Multiple dollars come back. It's the law of supply. I have seen this principle work so many times in my own life and in the lives of people around me.

Does this make sense to you? Does it connect with your life experience, as it does with mine?

We can open our eyes to the currency of miracles.

We are all familiar with a wonderful story in the Jewish tradition, the story of Chanukah. There was only enough oil to burn the lamps in the temple for a short time, but those lamps burned for a week. It's a miracle that tells us the news of God's willingness to provide for us. It is such a simple story. There are so many stories in the Jewish tradition that center on bravery, sacrifice, and other major issues of what it means to be alive on this earth. Yet the story of Chanukah, with its simple message about God's willingness to provide for us, is among the most elevated and the most celebrated.

When I was a little boy, I believed such stories. I believed that God could do whatever God wanted to do. Then I went to college, and then to seminary. And I stopped relating to miracle stories about this higher presence, and I stopped believing them. They were just parables or allegories. Those were the days when seminaries were involved in what we called "de-mythologizing" religious stories. The motivation for it was that contemporary people, people who were attending religious services, were becoming alienated by all the unrealistic talk about miracles and divine interventions. We were trying to become more current and more modern in those days. But in reality, we were taking all of the vigor and the power out of the very stories that could tell us about the higher spiritual powers that could be called upon to help us in our lives.

"These stories describe events that we know could not have happened," we told each other. "They cannot be literally true. We can relate to them only as symbolism. We can take lessons from them, but we cannot put them to real use in our lives."

But then the years passed. I experienced my own life challenges and troubles. As the leader of a large congregation, I came to share in the problems of many other people. And at some point, I became more and more aware that some higher power is at work in our lives. It has a unique way of interceding in our lives. This higher power, I discovered through many experiences, has a way, for those who trust in it, of meeting needs and making something from nothing.

We need to trust. The universal spiritual law is there. God does provide.

We can change the desire to be just a "taker."

When I was a boy, I once heard a minister say, "Everybody is either a giver or a taker." I didn't understand fully what he was talking about. I wanted to believe it at the time, perhaps because he punctuated his statement with a pointing finger and a thunderous, "Which one are you?"

Once I got past his accusatory tone, I realized he was probably right. Essentially, either we are givers or we are takers. There are those of us who, as you know, are totally takers. They are always asking, always seeking ways to get ahead, always making deals at the expense of other people. There are also many people who consistently position themselves on the giving side of the equation.

Most of us give some of the time, take at other times. Still, we tend to fall more into one camp or the other. If we tend to take more than we give, we need to be honest with ourselves. We need to overcome the fear of loss that keeps us from giving. If we are always giving too much, we need to look at that too, as Charles Barkley did. Perhaps we suffer from low self-esteem that makes us feel that by giving, we will be better liked. Or we have become victimized by relationships with people who unfairly take advantage of us, and we cannot find a healthy way to change them. Such problems of give and take require our attention if we are to build a healthy relationship to money and the real issues of welfare and bountifulness.

When I look at myself, I can see some of each trait. There are times when I am in a giving mode, and I am a good giver. I trust, and I get into the flow of giving. But there are times when I'm not. I find myself thinking, "What has this person done for me? Why am I acting on his or her behalf?"

We need to get beyond that kind of thinking. Giving is not a barter, not a quid pro quo. Only when we learn to give without expectation or justification can we open our hearts fully to what prosperity really means.

We can resist giving into the expectation of getting thanks or anything else in return.

The other morning as I was shaving and listening to a radio talk program, I heard a man being interviewed about his experiences as an emergency medical technician. He spent much of his time working on an ambulance. He was asked if he had ever had a chance to talk, afterward, to someone whose life he had saved.

I was expecting a heart-warming tale of tears and gratitude to follow. How could anyone not be filled with gratitude when meeting the one who had saved his or her life? But that is not the story I heard.

He told the interviewer that about a month earlier, his unit was called to a pizza parlor where the owner had had a heart attack. The man said that he had managed to revive the pizzeria owner and transport him to an emergency room, where his life was saved.

During a lunch hour a few weeks later, the medical technician and the other members of his team happened to be in the area again. So they went to the same pizza parlor, where they expected to be greeted like returning heroes.

That didn't happen! When the man entered, the man who had nearly died didn't say, "This is the man who saved my life!" Nor did he say, "I owe this man my life. Free pizza for everyone!" Instead, the pizzeria owner looked at the man who had saved his life and said, "I remember you. Hey Johnnie, give him a Coke on me!"

That is a funny story, but it illustrates a point. As I stood there listening to the radio, I was astonished at the pizzeria owner's attitude, and I thought, "This should have been a sacred moment. That man should have said, 'Because of you, I am here today. Bless you! I want to do something to honor you.' At the very least, the *very* least, he should have given everybody in the store a free slice of pizza in honor of this man!"

There are countless tales of ingratitude directed against people who try to do good for others, only to be rebuffed or hurt in return. Sometimes, it seems that life is like one of those sight gags in a movie in which a helpful person takes the arm of an elderly woman and attempts to help her across the street, only to receive a smashing blow across the head from the woman's purse.

Rather than judging others, I think we would do well to commit ourselves to thinking one bigger thought and to making one greater plan for our lives. We can commit to give because it is right to do so.

Deepening Our Understanding

It is nice to have material wealth. Certainly, having enough to live comfortably is preferable to living in a state of chronic need and want.

Yet amassing wealth for personal enjoyment is not the path to true prosperity. Giving of yourself is, making you more prosperous than holding back. Blessing is more important than receiving favors. Giving selflessly is more enriching than expecting favors, or even gratitude, in exchange. These are simple rules, but powerful.

It is often said that wealth can make you free. With money, you can own what you want, live where you want, go where you want, and do what you want. Those things may be true. But giving is even more powerful. Through giving, you will achieve the freedom to not only do what you want but also to evolve into an extraordinary force in the world and the lives of those around you. You will be uplifted, blessed, and free. And you will enjoy spiritual riches that will be greater than any assets found in any bank account, or even in all the banks in the world.

10

Freedom Follows Seeking Our Personal Truth

*I*n the last decade, more and more companies have discovered the value of creating mission statements that encapsulate in just a few words, their reason for being. On the heels of the popularity of mission statements, it seems that more and more individuals have been creating mission statements of their own.

It is a positive trend, but I would like to deepen it and extend it in ways that can make a more profound difference in our lives, lifting us to new levels of freedom and accomplishments. Because both beneath and above our missions for living—the things we would like to accomplish in our lives—there is another purpose we need to discover.

It is our personal truth. It encompasses more than simply what we want to get done. It also embodies our reasons for being here, for taking part in this human journey, during our rich and varied life experiences on this earth.

I once knew a man who was in a constant state of agitation. Over the course of years, I never saw him calm. As far as I know, he had no real reason to be agitated. He had been born into considerable wealth. In many ways, he had enjoyed an easy life. But despite what seemed to be good fortune, he was brimming with dissatisfaction and prejudice. I'd frequently hear him put people down or complain about what a difficult day he was having.

Then when he was very old and ill, he asked me to visit with him. Sensing death approaching, he was finally reflecting on his life. Whatever his motivation might have been, he wanted to talk.

When I arrived, he told me that when he was very young, he had great ambitions. Once, at a youth conference, he had a profoundly spiritual experience and made a commitment to God. He felt that some higher power had called him to accomplish something significant, something extraordinary, with his life.

He described the excitement of that time. How much good he planned to do! But at the end, reflecting back on the long years, he said, "I didn't do any of it." As we were talking, I thought again of what Thoreau had said—that the worst thing that can happen is to come to the end of our life and discover that we haven't really lived.

My sad friend had betrayed the best that was in him, and the result had been constant inner agitation. He had never known inner peace.

This man's story is not unusual. Many people, though they may dearly want inner peace, don't know how to find it. Other people, even after they seem to have accomplished a great deal in their lives, come to their last days with a thirst to accomplish something meaningful with their lives.

Our lives are varied. Each of us faces different challenges. Each of us brings a different set of skills to the process of living, and different values regarding what is meaningful and good. Yet all of us, despite those variables, share one thing:

For each of us, there is a personal truth, a reason why we were placed on this earth.

When we fail to search for that truth, we lose the part of life that may be the most valuable, and the most to be thirsted for, of all:

- *We give up our power to make a unique, individual impact on the world.* We can do "as well" as other people, or possibly "better" than other people. These goals, while valuable, are slight in comparison to what we can accomplish by seeking our individual truth. In that way, and that way alone, can we create something that is unique and entirely ours.

- *We remain dissatisfied.* Following the lead of other people rather than our inner truth, we are left forever hungering for something more. Our unique abilities in the world are never brought to light or put into action.

- *We are not free to accomplish all we can.* We are like the second or third riders in a bicycle race. We can do as well as the people who are ahead of us in the line. Living on our truth, in contrast, is like taking the lead. We can see no one before us. We are setting our own pace with power and determination. We are accomplishing something unique and lasting in the world. Our personal truth alone empowers us in that way.

How can we uncover our personal truth? Then, how can we *live* it?

We can start by recognizing that there is a call.

Wherever we are in our lives, there is always a call—a voice telling us where we should go next, where our hearts really want to go. For this reason, I believe there is not just one calling in life.

Some people may be engaged in busy careers, but hearing a call to become parents. Conversely, some of us are busy parents who hear a call to go back to work, resume our careers. I know one woman, a successful lawyer, who made the decision to become a social worker and help people in a different way. I also know a very accomplished and successful cellist who has felt a strong impulse to become a teacher.

One of my own sons, from his earliest years, felt a call to become a ferry boat captain. He did. Only recently, an injury forced him from that kind of work, and he is now exploring other calls and ways to move his life, and his work, in new directions.

Our hearts pull us this way and that, and we would do well to heed the messages they bring us. I believe that voice is calling to us in our lives every day. It summons us to find our personal truth. And there is something curious about it. Unless we understand that voice that is seeking us, we will never seek it. Once we know it is there, we have taken the first step toward claiming our unique gifts as human beings.

We can make an active decision to start the process of seeking our truth.

We can discover the reason we were born, the purpose for our being. Just as our fingerprints are all different, every single person has a different soul imprint. There is a purpose for every soul brought onto the face of this world. When your whole being is focused around this search, you have taken the vital first steps on a journey that will lead to inner peace and freedom.

What is the purpose of your life?

What are you here to do?

These are core questions. If you don't deal with them, they have a way of dealing with you.

Do you believe, as I do, that the higher power makes no mistakes, that the universe has a purpose for each of us, for every human life? If you do, you owe it to yourself to search for your unique purpose.

We can get beyond words.

As a person who speaks often in public and who also has to prepare many sermons each year, I am about to offer some advice that might seem paradoxical and strange:

> *Your inner truth will not be revealed in words alone, nor can it always be expressed in oral or written statements. It might be a sensation of love, or a vision, or a piece of music or sound, or even a matrix made up of all these, or more.*

Often, our truth is revealed to us in what might be called an *epiphany*: an experience or sensation that elevates us to some new place in our lives. So many people experience epiphanies, it is surprising to me that the recognition of their prevalence and power has not entered into mainstream thinking or writings today.

Epiphanies are all around us:

- A professional musician I know tells me that music took over his life when he was a young man. He was standing by a piano as a neighbor of his played a simple song. With no decision on his part, the rest of his life seemed to take shape before him. Tears began to roll down his cheeks and his path became clear.

- A Muslim Imam I know tells me too that his vision to follow his faith did not result from a structured, planned series of decisions. He went to a mosque, saw people worship, and felt as though he were being swept up, physically and mentally, to some new place where he had never been before, a place that was right for him. No one had said to him, "You have to work out a purpose for your life! You have to write down a mission statement and put it on the wall!" Life placed a unique experience, a unique truth, before him.

- A man I know explains that he had never thought too much about the idea of becoming a parent. Then his first son was born and his life was suddenly lifted to a new, higher purpose he could not even put into words. Love took him over—a profound and life-changing love that was really a revelation of personal truth.

We can discuss what truth means. We can make lists. We can talk to wise counselors about what we ought to be doing in our lives. All those activities are important. But unless we are vulnerable to influxes of sudden, unexpected meaning in our lives, we can never attain our full growth as human beings.

We can invite a spiritual presence into our search.

The Austrian psychiatrist Viktor Frankl had much to say about this topic. I love the depth of his mind, the quality of his expression, and the understanding he brings to life.

Viktor Frankl was a survivor of a Nazi concentration camp. In his writing, he describes the absolute worst human behavior. He was witness to horrors that most of us will never see. Yet he also tells us that even in places of ultimate destruction, he saw the greatest human behavior. He witnessed acts of wondrous kindness and humanity.

In his book *Unheard Cry for Meaning* (Simon & Schuster, 1979), Viktor Frankl talks about how, at the age of 15, he developed what he called an "operational definition" of his relationship to God, which he returned to more and more often in his later life:

> *When you are talking to yourself in utmost sincerity and ultimate solitude, he to whom you're addressing yourself may be justifiably called God.*

This is a rare insight. The person whom we are addressing in our inmost thoughts is not ourselves. It is God.

I find this happening often, even among atheists, agnostics, and people who place very little stock in religion. I furthermore believe that such a serious, profound inner dialogue has to be connected to some kind of true spirituality.

At our very core, at the foundation of who we are, there it is! Yes, we are flesh and blood. Yes, we live in a material world. But our essence is spiritual. At our core, our truth resides at the place where we exist as souls.

We can seek out true wisdom, the wisdom passed down through the ages.

In our search for personal truth, we need to seek out true wisdom—wisdom that has endured the tests of time, wisdom that has been shown to work time and time again through history.

Unless we orient ourselves in this way, to genuine sources of insight, we are often blown about like petals in a spring storm.

Rather than turning to the latest religious or self-help fads, we can connect to tried and true sources of wisdom. And because, as I mentioned earlier, our personal truth can be discovered not only in words, we can seek many different sources of wisdom:

- Membership in a religious or spiritual community.

- Encounters with great literature, music, and paintings.

- New life encounters through travel, friendships, walks in nature, and other rich experiences.

- Readings of the great texts from all great world religions.

Yes, we might find wisdom and self-knowledge by watching television, listening to the radio, and reading newspapers and magazines. But how deep is that knowledge? How much of it really works?

We can take responsibility for ourselves.

"Oh yes," you might say, "but isn't that awfully difficult?"

Yes, it is difficult to take responsibility for ourselves. So many of us would like to go back to being little children, allowing our parents to take care of us, answer all our questions, and meet our every need. But if we are to encounter our personal truth, we cannot delegate the process away.

So many of us resist taking on that responsibility for our own lives and challenges. Some of us even misuse the services of psychotherapists, relying upon them to identify and solve our most pressing life problems for us. Of course, good psychologists will not attempt to do that for us—they help us bring our problems into the light of day, then act as guides who help direct us to the hard work we need to do to solve them.

When we see that we did something wrong or mishandled something in our lives, they often say we can point a blaming finger at our parents or our childhood environment or the opportunities we didn't have. We can always find an excuse to say, "I don't have to take responsibility for what I have become. It was not my fault."

Instead, we can choose another path. Rather than using our knowledge of human nature to excuse ourselves from responsibility for our lives, we can use our new knowledge to better understand ourselves. We can actually take *greater* responsibility for who we are and who we have become.

The writer Erica Jong has a very pithy comment about this. She once remarked that when we take our lives fully into our own hands, a terrible thing happens to us: We have no one to blame!

You and I cannot fully deal with why we were born or our personal truths until we take responsibility for the givens of our lives and confront the challenges of facing down our own problems. In fact, we often begin to discern our personal truth only when we:

- Take responsibility for our health conditions.

- Establish success in our careers so we do not depend on others.

- Exercise and tend to the maintenance of our bodies.

- Attend responsibly to the needs of our children, parents, spouses, partners, and friends.

These tasks might seem burdensome, but in practice they are not. In responsibility, we gain the freedom to discover all that we can become.

We can take personal responsibility for the search instead of blaming other people for our problems.

One of the more engrossing books I have read in recent years is *My American Journey* by Colin Powell (Random House, 1995). General Powell's modesty, humor, and humility shine from every page. It is a book that was clearly written by a true leader.

Before I read this book, I was not aware that General Powell was born to Jamaican parents who had left the Caribbean and moved to the Bronx, where young Colin was raised. From the earliest days, it was clear that he was a boy of exceptional ability. Perhaps because he loved America so much for the opportunities he found here, he decided at an early age to become a soldier—to fight and protect the homeland that his family found so dear.

So he did indeed become a soldier, but became an officer at a very dire time in our nation's history. He went to Vietnam. And while he was there, he became extremely disillusioned with life in the military. It was a time when the U.S. military routinely inflated the body counts of Vietnamese casualties. It was a time when Powell had colleagues die literally in his arms, for reasons he was forced to call into question. It was also a time when he witnessed pointless, horrid death raining down upon an often helpless civilian population.

Many men turned their disillusionment over Vietnam into lifelong bitterness toward America. But not Powell. Instead, he renewed his patriotism—even his love of the Army—and vowed to take a higher path.

Here are the words he uses in *My American Journey* to describe this transformation:

> *Many of my generation, the career captains, majors, and lieutenant colonels seasoned in that war, vowed that when our turn came to call the shots, we would not quietly acquiesce in halfhearted warfare for half-baked reasons that the American people could not understand or support. If we could make good on that promise to ourselves . . . then the sacrifices of Vietnam would not have been in vain.*

And, of course, we now know what a glorious career General Powell has had, and how he fulfilled this statement. Instead of blaming others and dropping out of what he sees as a glorious participation in American life, he shouldered responsibility for his own actions and moved his life to a higher plane.

We can remember to be lighthearted, not grim, in our search.

The words "seek personal truth!" seem to embody a rather ponderous, serious tone. Yet as I draw to the end of this chapter, let me observe that without happiness and joy, we can rarely draw close to that truth. If we work too hard and are grim in our search, the truth often flies away from us before we can capture it or examine its inestimable worth.

This is one reason why, when thinking of my truth and central reason for being here, I think of the story told by George Reavis in his wonderful children's book, *The Animal School* (Crystal Springs Books, 1999). It might be called another "Animal Farm." Let me summarize the story for you.

Once upon a time, the animals decided they had to do something heroic to meet the problems of life in "a new world." So they organized a school. They adopted a curriculum consisting of running, climbing, swimming, and flying. To make it easier to administer the curriculum, all the animals took all the subjects.

The duck was excellent in swimming, better than his instructor, but he made only passing grades in flying and was very bad at running. Since he was slow when running, he had to stay after school and he also had to drop swimming in order to practice running. This was kept up until his webbed feet were badly worn from running, and he had become only average in swimming. But average was acceptable in that school, so nobody worried, except the duck!

The rabbit started at the top of the class in running but nearly had a nervous breakdown because he had to do so much remedial work in swimming. The squirrel was excellent in climbing until he developed frustration in flying class where his teacher made him start from the ground up instead of from the treetop down. He earned a C in climbing and a D in running.

The eagle was a problem child and was disciplined severely. In the climbing class, he beat all the others to the top of the tree, but he insisted on using his own way to get there.

At the end of the year, an eel was the valedictorian. He could swim exceedingly well, and he could also run, climb, and fly a little. Overall, he had achieved the highest average.

Have you felt forced toward mediocrity, like these animals? Have you ever felt like an eel? I know that I have. Far from encouraging people to discover their unique gift, our society often gives people a hard time when they try to discover what their truth is all about.

Deepening Our Understanding

There is something we need to pursue in our lives. It is our personal truth, our reason for being present here on this earth. We might glimpse this truth in our mission statements, our priorities, and our goals, but only incompletely. Our personal truth might encompass those elements, but it goes deeper and higher and wider and further. It is really as close as we can possibly draw to understanding *who we are.*

When we live our lives in the search for this truth, surprising things happen in our lives:

- *We begin to make a unique, highly individual impact on the world.* We create new categories for what can be done—both by ourselves and by others.

- *We enjoy life more and discover the true satisfaction of living.* We sense our lives are making a difference, that we are making a permanent difference in the lives of others and a permanent mark on the world. Like that lead rider in the bicycle race I mentioned at the beginning of this chapter, we see a new road unfolding. The wind is behind us, and we are truly, finally free.

In the end, our personal truth is not a single idea, or a set of words, or even a picture we draw. It is a process, continuously evolving. It could be described as a never-ending surprise. The surprise of becoming free.

11

Freedom Follows Trusting

---

*W*hen I was a little child, I remember standing on the third or fourth step of the staircase in our house. My father was standing below, saying, "Jump, Arthur, jump!"

I hesitated. Would I be safe? Would he catch me? He kept assuring me it was safe to go ahead and jump. I was filled with mixed emotions. Finally I overcame my fears enough to throw myself into the air toward my father. I remember the indescribable feeling of relief and exhilaration as his strong arms caught me and I nestled safely against him.

In life, countless situations call upon us to trust other people, to trust fate, to trust God, to trust that we can enter into the unknown, despite the uncertainties, the risks, and our inner hesitations and fears. Without the willingness to trust, we are not free to act in many critical areas of our lives. We stay stuck in safe areas, never moving forward, not free to move ahead into new areas of our lives.

The other day, while riding in an airplane flying at 30,000 feet, I had a stark and sudden realization. I was trusting my life to the pilot! I knew nothing about him, beyond the sound of his voice. I couldn't even remember his name because I had not been paying close attention when he made his customary welcoming announcement to us over the sound system. Yet I was there, trusting my life to him.

I realized that I was lacking a lot of other important information about the situation I was in. Who were the mechanics who checked the plane before it took off? Who had put in the fuel? Who had performed the routine maintenance? For that matter, who were the air traffic controllers who were watching that little blip on their tracking screens, that little blip that contained my life and the lives of my fellow passengers? Were those controllers on top of the situation, or were they distracted? The awareness of how much trust we often put in complete strangers really came home to me.

But when we stop to think for only a moment, we realize that our well-being is dependent on so many assumptions that we would never be able to act at all if we lacked trust. Consider how immobilized we would be if we decided it was too risky to trust anyone:

- When we meet someone, fall in love, and decide to develop our relationships further, we trust so many things. At the most basic level, is the person we love really just who he or she claims to be? Are all the things that person tells us really true? Is that person honest and reliable? Even after years of a committed relationship or marriage, we are still required to trust that our partners are honest, faithful to us, and so many other things. Without trust, we would never be able to love.

- When we went to school, or to college or university, we placed great trust in the institution we had chosen. Without having any proof, we believed that the school was able to provide the training or learning we expected and needed. So without trust, we could never learn.

- When we apply for new jobs, we trust many things. We're counting on our new employer to have enough money in its accounts to pay us and cover the costs of health care and other benefits they offer to provide. We're counting on the management of that company to remain competitive in business so that we can have continuous employment. We count on the company to screen our fellow employees so we will not work in the company of dangerous or dishonest people. Without trust in the unknown, we would be unable to work or earn a livelihood.

- When we drive automobiles, we trust that the other drivers will observe the rules of the road. They will stop at stoplights and not run into us. They will not drive under the influence of alcohol. We also trust that road engineers have created bridges, tunnels, and roads that are well designed and safe. Without a rich mosaic of overlapping trusts and confidences, we could never drive.

On and on this list could go. The message is clear. Without trust, we would be powerless to act in the world. We could not even sit calmly at home because even there we have placed trust in the electricians who installed our wires and the roofers who put shingles over our heads.

When we stop to think about trust in this way, we see that it is a bigger problem than we realized. Some readers of this book might also have had a sudden realization as they read the last few pages of this book:

Yes, trust is more of a challenge for me than I realized. It does have me immobilized in areas I have not recognized.

Trust is indeed a powerful force. Yet where do we go for help to find it? How can we gain the security within to dare to trust others?

We can start by admitting that we have a problem with the issue of trusting.

Earlier in this book, I observed that Alcoholics Anonymous and other successful 12-step programs all start their healing processes by requiring people to admit that they have a problem. There is a very practical reason for this. Unless we admit that we have a problem, we can never begin to do all the difficult work that is needed to process it and remove it from our lives.

Part of the problem may be that we equate trusting with being naïve. When we trust, we fear we will be taken advantage of or appear unsophisticated.

How do we discover where this problem, this lack of trust, is at work? We start by looking at specific areas of our lives where we feel unhappy, agitated, and unfulfilled. Only by examining them closely can we start to pinpoint the areas where we are crippling ourselves by failing to trust. Some of these areas might be these:

- *You worry a great deal that you are being taken advantage of in many areas of your life.* When you hire a technician to make repairs in your home, you obsess that she or he is charging too much, doing shoddy work, or charging more than someone else might have. When you buy a new automobile, you cannot sleep because you are worrying so much that you paid more than you might have at another car dealer. Of course, it is important to be careful in life, to make good selections and good choices. But when you are obsessing about things you cannot possibly control, you have encountered a place in your life where it would be healthy to try to let go and trust more.

- *You obsess that people are not telling you the truth.* Perhaps you've lent your car to your teenage son and told him he can only go to a party on the other side of your town, not drive to other towns. But when he leaves, you worry that he is not actually going where he said he was going. Or perhaps you are obsessing that a business partner is not being truthful with you. Or perhaps you have become jealous about your spouse or partner, worrying excessively that he or she is becoming attracted to others.

Of course, some of the scenarios I have just described can represent very troubling problems in our lives. But the fact is, failing to trust will never be the tool that solves them. Failing to trust only makes the problems worse. It is a false remedy we use to distract ourselves from taking the steps we need to take to solve the problems. If we fear our partner or spouse is not being forthright with us, for example, we need to discuss that problem and bring it into the light of day. If we feel we cannot trust our children, we need to find appropriate ways to discuss that with them and set up procedures and rules that protect both them, and us, from harm.

We can build our ability to trust.

If you have realized that you have a difficult time trusting others, it can be very productive to "test the waters" and experiment with new ways to broaden our ability to trust. Trust, like a muscle, can be strengthened through exercises like these:

- *Get to know better the person, or persons, you are having a difficult time trusting.* If you distrust a colleague or business partner, for example, increase the frequency and quality of your communication with him or her. Ask about issues and problems that lie outside the area where you are having a problem with trusting, such as personal interests and family life. By getting a more rounded view of that other person, you will be able to judge better whether he or she is trustworthy and whether you have been guilty of distrusting unnecessarily.

- *Extend trust in small ways and see it come back to you.* If you have a troubled, untrusting relationship with a teenage son or daughter, find a safe way for him or her to demonstrate trustworthiness to you. Remember, the key concept is *safe*. It can be an invitation to disaster to say, "Here's the car. Take it for the weekend." Or "Dad and I will be out of town all weekend. Why not invite some friends over Saturday night?" But with a little thought, you can place trust in that son or daughter. Your children can go off to special (well-supervised) summer programs, get jobs, and perform volunteer work at hospitals and nursing homes. As I say, stretching your ability to trust can repay you with surprising rewards.

We can go to the source of so much help and wisdom—our religious and spiritual traditions.

In my own tradition, I go to the Bible, which I sometimes refer to as "the wisdom book." It embodies the light and the wisdom, the common sense, of centuries of time. It is God's presentation of the big ideas that are essential if we are to enjoy good and abundant lives.

And the Bible is the perfect place to go to learn about trust. In seeking to learn the art of trusting, a great place to spend time is in the Psalms, which are a part of both our Jewish and Christian traditions. In them, you will discover focused advice about an extraordinarily wide range of human experience:

- Anger

- Confusion

- Despair

- Hatred

- Envy

- Self-pity

That is quite an extensive list of problems. Most interesting of all is that, when you stop to think about them individually, each one turns out to have strong connections to the issue of trust. A lack of trust, in fact, can trigger any of those problems, and trigger it quickly.

We know that David wrote most of the Psalms, and we admire his wonderful, poetic language. David knows, and tells us, that when we are faithful to God, God responds without fail. Every time.

As you read through the Psalms, you will notice that they are all really penetrating meditations about our relationship with God. Trust is fundamental to the health of that relationship, and we need trust to bring all the good things of God into our lives.

You will also notice that David struggles with doubt, much as we do today. Then, when he voices his conviction that God is always there for us, he is actually rising out of the depths of despair and doubt to rediscover and reassert his faith.

How often do we also go through just such struggles and restatements of faith? Very often.

Then, in Psalm 37, David speaks with the certainty of one who has tested his faith repeatedly and come back stronger, and more trusting, each time. In Verse 3, he tells us:

Trust God and do good so you will live in the land with security.

That is quite a promise. Yet it tells us that we not only learn to trust by acting passively. We also need to act. We need to do good and be honest.

By being kind, fair, generous, loving, and forgiving, your life will be enriched. First, every time you live by the highest principles, you reinforce the goodness that is in you. It strengthens you and makes you whole. Second, when you start a cycle of love and kindness, you will find they come back to you. You will be rewarded with similar responses from others. It is a spiritual law, a practical reality, that we get back what we give.

Then, in Verse 4, we find these words:

Take delight in the Lord. And the Lord will give you the desires of your heart.

That is an incredible promise, that if you take pleasure in God, as you think and read about God, and as you pray, taking delight in the interaction, you're going to get caught up with something wonderful. Lighten up and start delighting in God! When you do that, in God's own way, in God's own time, God has a way of giving you the desires of your heart. But you've got to trust God to have that experience.

We can make a commitment to place our trust in some higher power.

Make a commitment that you will trust God; trust that higher power, no matter what. Without variation, you will trust that God's actions will be in your best interests. This change in outlook may require a leap of faith for you.

To initiate this process, you will find that it is important to set aside your intellect. Trusting in some higher power is more than an action of your mind. It is a letting go of your whole self. It is a releasing, an abandonment of self to trust. It is surrendering yourself to the arms of a loving and attentive higher power who will reward your trust in ways you will never imagine.

We can take personal responsibility for our own happiness.

The other day I was having lunch in a restaurant when the waiter brought me a little card from a woman at another table. On the front was the image of an angel with wings extended, a quarter moon, and some stars. I opened it and liked what I read:

> *If you really want to be happy, nobody can stop you. Happiness is an inside job.*

That made sense to me. Nobody can ruin your happiness. They can upset it, they can temporarily displace it, but nobody can take your happiness away from you. We need to trust these realities.

The issues of happiness and trust are closely intertwined. Often, we accuse other people of being untrustworthy as a way to justify and increase our own unhappiness. We say, "I would be happy if only I could rely upon . . ."

Other people can enhance your happiness, they can complete it, they can make it wonderful. But you cannot assign to somebody else the responsibility of making you happy. You can't go to somebody else and say, "It's your job to give me happiness." We try to do that sometimes when we're young and in love—even when we're old and in love. But it doesn't work.

Not long ago, I came across an insight on happiness from the Catholic thinker and essayist Agnes Repplier, who wrote in her book *Essays in Miniature* (Scholarly Press, 1970):

> *It is not easy to find happiness in ourselves, and it is not possible to find it elsewhere.*

We can keep a healthy perspective.

A number of years ago I befriended a man of great soul, whose temperament was a shining example of understanding just this reality, that nothing can be achieved without perspective and trust. He was the late Pete McCulley, a journeyman coach in professional football. When in New York, Pete was a coach with the New York Jets. Pete, a man of great faith and energy, was always energetic and upbeat. Once, when the Jets were having a bad year, I called him to commiserate after one particularly dismal loss. Pete was not downhearted. He said:

> *You know, Arthur, there were 900 million people in China who didn't even know we played today! How about that?*

Pete had perspective. He was in the flow. In him, I saw something reflected that John Wesley was talking about when he said:

> *Work as if everything depends on you. Pray as if everything depends on God.*

When you do that, in that order—you do your very best, you put all your energy into it, and then pray—your prayers transcend. You get in the flow of the spirit, and some higher power takes over.

Some of you will surely remember the name Roy Campanella. He was a Hall of Fame catcher for the old Brooklyn Dodgers. One of the first American blacks to get into major league baseball, he was on the same team as Jackie Robinson and was as beloved and valuable.

In the midst of his career, he was in an automobile accident that left him a quadriplegic. He did most of his rehabilitation work at the famous Rusk Institute for Rehabilitative Medicine in New York. Commenting on his situation, he said, "We quads are a hearty breed. We know how to overcome and keep on living." Often, as he wheeled through the corridors of Rusk Institute he went by a plaque, and one day he stopped to look at it. It's called, "A Creed For Those Who Have Suffered," written by an unknown Confederate soldier:

> *I asked God for strength, that I might achieve. I was made weak, that I might learn humbly to obey . . .*
>
> *I asked for health, that I might do great things. I was given infirmity, that I might do better things . . .*
>
> *I asked for riches, that I might be happy. I was given poverty, that I might be wise . . .*
>
> *I asked for power, that I might have the praise of men. I was given weakness, that I might feel the need of God . . .*
>
> *I asked for all things, that I might enjoy life. I was given life, that I might enjoy all things . . .*
>
> *I got nothing I asked for—but everything I had hoped for. Almost despite myself, my unspoken prayers were answered. I am, among men, most richly blessed!*

Whatever your religious tradition, try to cultivate that level of trust in some higher power in the universe. Trust that something higher than you will take care of you and give you what you need. And when that happens, you will have achieved a level of freedom and happiness that no one can take away from you.

There is another comment too that I would like to add here—a curious one, I have to admit. It is that many of us find it difficult to also trust when things are going well in our lives. Everything seems to be working, yet some inner voice calls to us, saying, "Be careful! Just when things seem to be going well, that is when the worst things are likely to occur!"

I refute that kind of thinking. When my grandchildren are about to come to visit me, I trust that I will have a wonderful experience with them. And I always do. When I am about to go to dinner with friends, I trust that it will be a warm, fulfilling evening. And this kind of trust works too. It is a powerful way to capture the joy of our daily lives.

Deepening Our Understanding

When we cannot trust others, we give away our freedom to act in so many ways. Consider that, after all, no great things can be achieved by one person working entirely alone. The space shuttle is commanded not by one person but by a team. A symphony can be performed only by a conductor and many instrumentalists. A family may be headed by one person, but of course no one person can ever be in charge.

Unless we learn to trust others, to build our ability to trust, we can never be free to achieve great things.

12

Freedom Follows Courage

*D*o you know who you really are? Do you know where you really come from and what you're all about? Are you aware of all the strengths, all the talents, and all the gifts that are in you? Do you actively experience how unique you are?

Courage will open those doors for you. If there's any great sin that we create for ourselves, it is that we don't have enough confidence in ourselves. Too often, we are like shrinking violets, not showing the real fullness of who we are. We limit ourselves because of our fear to act. We keep ourselves from exercising the real freedoms we already possess, the latitude we really have that can help us achieve our needed growth.

Through bravery, we encounter ourselves. Like trust, courage is a tool we need to push back the boundary between who we are and who we will become.

Courage means to have heart, to operate from the core and heart of who we are. It helps to be reminded that life begins with a heartbeat and ends when the heart stops. Our heart indeed is at our center and at the core of our human existence. When we live our lives with courage, we are literally living with our heart. We are putting all of our heart, the best of us, into the process of living.

Whatever you are facing, if you put your heart—the best of you—into it, you will be living a life of courage.

Sir Winston Churchill once said that courage is the first of human qualities, because it is the one that makes all others possible.

When we think of courage, physical courage usually comes to mind first. How often, for instance, do we hear on the news that a firefighter has died in the line of duty? How many times, in the wake of the attacks on the World Trade Center, were we astonished and moved by the accounts of the heroic actions taken by firefighters?

I am always awed by the way firefighters will go into burning buildings time after time as if they didn't understand the danger. But they do understand the danger, and they still do it.

Courage is certainly a requirement of being on the police force as well. Every moment that our law enforcement professionals are in uniform, they are facing a world of danger and violence.

I was raised during World War II. Those of us living during that era heard of one miracle after another. Each newspaper brought new stories of men and women who had sacrificed their lives for others. I was fortunate to have grown up with that kind of influence because we need these demonstrations of courage as role models to get inspired to stretch ourselves.

When we avoid courage, we harm ourselves in so many ways:

- *We thwart our own growth and remain stuck in older, outmoded self-definitions.* Do you know people who have not grown substantially since they were young? They can be very sad people indeed, and most often, their lack of progress has resulted from a lack of courage to move ahead in areas of education, enterprise, and relationships.

- *Our lives become repetitive because we keep repeating tasks we have performed in the past.* Instead of trying to change jobs or get a promotion, some of us find it safer to go to the same desk every day and perform the same tasks. Instead of trying to gain acceptance into a top college or university, some young people prefer to take the easier route and apply to schools where they know they can get in and where they will not be challenged.

Acting with courage is not easy, but in the end, it represents the higher road—the right thing to do. Courage is the recipe for growth. How can we bring the power of courage to work in our lives?

We can admit that we are afraid.

I am not talking about fear in the face of terrible, life-threatening danger. We all see depictions of that kind of fear in popular movies and television shows. Perhaps a young soldier gets the order to advance in battle with other soldiers but wavers, saying, "Do I have the courage to do what I am being asked to do?"

Engaging as those depictions of courage may be, they have little to do with the kind of courage we need to advance our lives. How often do we confront situations that are truly a matter of life or death? Probably not on a daily basis.

But we do confront danger, perhaps more often than we realize. Some of us go to work every day for organizations that are downsizing. We live in danger of being fired—a very real danger indeed. Others of us drive to our jobs on dangerous, crowded highways, often forgetting the peril we face. Still others of us need to be constantly cognizant of medical problems we face. Without our medication or our routines, we are in peril.

So the kind of courage I am talking about is felt in countless smaller ways as we go about our daily lives. In sum, it adds up to more than the great courage we are sometimes required to exhibit at cataclysmic moments.

I remember a sad conversation I had some time ago with a frustrated and unhappy man. He was bright and gifted, with wonderful personal skills, yet he had not done much with his life. He hadn't finished college, and he had never taken a job that challenged him.

"Why do you think this happened?" I asked.

"Fear," he answered. "I was afraid."

He told me a story much like one I have heard countless times from many other people. "Everybody in my family was successful," he said. "My parents were high achievers. My siblings were all doing well. I felt that if I were to try to rise to the same level, I might fail. So I decided to do nothing. Because I was afraid to risk, I'm in a mess today."

I think fear causes more damage, creates more problems, produces more unhappiness, than anything else in human experience. In fact, it may be accurate to consider fear to be our number 1 enemy. It's like a virus. When it enters into our system, it never goes away. Once it is there, it keeps eating away at us, taking away our energy, motivation, and happiness. It keeps pulling us down.

Fear prevents us from doing the courageous thing. We consider the possible consequences, and we don't do what we should.

Fear also blocks our creativity. There are things we would love to do, but we do not do them because we are afraid of criticism, judgment, and failure. Because it is so much easier, we put our lives on hold.

What do we do with our fears? What do we do with these pesky little demons—this virus that gets into the psyche and works against us—keeps us saying "no, no, not now" and makes us hold back?

We can then stand up to fear.

If you can screw up the courage to face your fears and stare them down, in time they will begin to dissipate and disappear.

In other words, it is important to take a stand. Don't allow your fears to bully you. Because in all practical ways, fear is really a bully. I learned a great lesson about bullies when I was younger, from an unlikely source. It was from Tillinger, a little dog my son had when he was young. This little mutt was macho. He thought he was king of the universe. There was no dog he would not take on! Then once, when I was walking with Tillinger trotting along by my side, a tiny kitten came out from under a porch. Tillinger backed off, yelping with fear. He rubbed against me as if to say, "Daddy, take care of me. I'm scared."

That got me thinking. If Tillinger had stood his ground and barked, the kitten would have run away. I wonder if some of the fears that seem to be monsters are really kittens. Stand up. Face the fears. Stare them down. You will find it easier if you remember you are not alone. At your side is a divine power that will surround you, lift you up, and carry you. Whatever your religion or beliefs may be, remember that you don't have to do it alone.

We can remember that we have what it takes.

Several years ago, the New York Yankees were playing baseball as well as they have been for some time now. A friend invited me to attend a Yankee game with him. Because he was an acquaintance of George Steinbrenner, the principal owner of the Yankees, we had special seats at the stadium. My friend decided to make the night truly memorable and, over my objections, insisted on sending a car to pick me up and drive me to and from the game.

At six o'clock on the day of the game, a long white stretch limousine pulled up to get me. It was a very impressive sight, and I admit I did look quickly around to see if any neighbors were watching me get in. Then when the game was over, we returned to the limousine. The driver opened the door for us, and we climbed on board in regal fashion. We were inching our way down the street, which was teeming with people coming out of the stadium, when a little boy came up to the window, cupped his hands around his eyes, and looked inside. "Hey, mister," he asked. "Are you a somebody?"

I never got a chance to answer because the driver sped up and we were on our way. But I would have liked to say:

Son, if you think I'm a somebody in terms of being rich and famous, I am not. But am I a somebody? Yes, I am. And you're a somebody too. You are a unique human being. Nobody in the world has your fingerprints. Better yet, nobody has your soulprint. You were created by a power who loved you into life. That power, that force, never makes a mistake in bringing a soul to this earth. God wanted you to be.

If I could sit down with that little boy today, I'd talk about the creation story in Genesis, how God created the moon, the stars, the earth, the lakes, the oceans, the trees, and the animals—everything on the earth—and then God created a man and a woman. And God said, "It is good!" In effect, God was saying, "I like what I have created." And, as the story goes, God breathed breath into every living soul.

God has given us life. If we believe in God, we will believe in ourselves. When we need to muster up the courage to do anything, we will have the heart and strength and resources to do what we need to do.

We can stretch our abilities to practice bravery.

In every one of us there is a much bigger person than we give ourselves credit for. In fact, each of us has a giant inside. There are areas in all of our lives where we could experience incredible breakthroughs if only we had the courage to act. Yet despite the fact that these areas hold great potential to enable us to make real progress in our lives, we hold back. How can we muster up the courage to do the things we know we need to do in order to move our lives forward?

Popular Broadway musicals seem to offer many suggestions, possibly because they present so many situations in which people are trying to do brave things. *The King and I* offers one of the most famous songs that offer advice on the subject. "Whistle a Happy Tune" tells us that even the simplest act alleviates our fear and equips us to act more bravely. I believe that there is a reason why this song has become famous and beloved while so many others have been forgotten. "Whistle a Happy Tune" has staying power because it contains an element of fundamental truth, something that speaks to all of us. It tells us that when we act in a way that makes us appear unconcerned about danger, we in fact become more heroic.

Many years ago when I was serving at a church in Brooklyn, New York, I knew a woman who had embellished the message of that song with her own special, spiritual twist. Because she didn't want fear to prevent her from coming to evening meetings at church, she would sing hymns out loud as she walked back home through some pretty dangerous streets. She felt her inner bravery increase. She believed that her singing fended off people who might have wanted to harm her. In any case, she felt strengthened by the spirit of her singing and was less afraid.

There is another Broadway play that comes to mind where bravery is concerned. It is *Damn Yankees* with its famous song, "You Gotta Have Heart." We all know the words:

> *You gotta have heart, lots and lots and lots of heart.*

Again, there is a reason why this song has become so beloved. It is always sung with gusto, and that's appropriate because the word *courage* comes from the same root as the word *heart*. When we put our hearts into something, we find we have the courage to do what we need to do.

We see this in the Scriptures as well. At one point, when Jesus found that his disciples were discouraged in their attempts at prayer, he said, "Do not lose heart!" Jesus knew that if the disciples believed deep within themselves that God was interested in them, they would be heartened. They would gain the courage to live effectively and confidently.

We can cultivate the habit of practicing bravery in countless small ways.

I remember one July afternoon in Maine many years ago. My older brother had asked me to take his weekend guests around Casco Bay. I was using my younger son's boat because mine was too small to hold everyone. It had been a very pleasant afternoon. Because I wanted to show everyone Admiral Richard Byrd's island home, I set the course for home by a new route. Admiral Byrd, you know, was the first person to reach the North Pole.

We were in unfamiliar waters. I proceeded very cautiously as the Maine coast is mostly ledge, and it is easy to run aground in waters you do not know well. That afternoon, I felt I was doing well up that point. Finally, as I was approaching a part of the bay I was familiar with, I spotted a huge sailboat several hundred yards ahead of us. Knowing that boat had a keel much deeper than ours, I lined myself up and sailed behind. If I followed, I could have no problems! So I put the throttle ahead, going about 20 knots, and I commented to one of my brother's friends, "We're doing fine. The depth indicator shows we have 20 feet of water!" Not a second after, there was a tremendous crash.

We had hit a ledge! Everybody went reeling—except for me, because I was holding onto the wheel. My older brother fell into the lower cabin. I heard a man in the stern say, "My back! My back!" My older son, Paul, who was to be married on the next Saturday, was bleeding from his head. Something terrible had happened.

The boat was listing sharply to the right as water gushed into the lower cabin. For a long moment we were all frozen in place, and then my son had the quick wit to grab the radio and yell, "Mayday! Mayday!" Since it was a summer Saturday, boats were all around us to take off the injured people.

I was scared. I didn't know how badly people were hurt. I was concerned that the boat would sink. We were parked there on the ledge.

The next day, I went through one of the most difficult experiences of my life. I stood in the hospital corridor outside the room of the man who had badly injured his back because of my error. I was afraid to face him because of what I had done, afraid to face the fact that I should have stopped and studied a chart, that I shouldn't have gone so fast, that I should have been more careful. But the accident had happened. I was responsible for injury and damage.

Many times before these events, I had been called upon to visit people injured in accidents. On those occasions, I had always asked, "Did the person responsible ever call or come to see you?" Most of the time the people who had been injured would tell me that no, the person responsible had never expressed that level of concern. I remembered the judgment I had felt toward those people for not having the courage to face up to what they had done. Now I was that person. I could understand why people did not contact the people they had injured. It is a very difficult thing to do.

At last, I screwed up my courage and entered the room. I was hoping my injured friend would say, "Oh, Arthur, don't worry. These things happen. It's all right!" But he didn't say that. He was so angry with me. I had ruined his weekend, maybe his summer, and possibly his health. Fortunately, as it turned out, he recovered, but at the time we both knew I might have ruined a big portion of his life. It was a real possibility.

I can still remember how immobilized I felt standing in that hallway, outside that room. Fear is an overwhelmingly powerful force. It has an enormous effect on our lives. Yet we also know that courage is the antidote to fear. Courage! I learned an important lesson about courage, and about fear, when I talked with that man.

One important lesson I learned is that courage doesn't always result in immediate resolutions. It doesn't sweep problems away at once, in one magic stroke. The rewards of courage don't always follow immediately behind. Sometimes, you have to wait a long, long time for courageous acts to repay you. But in the end, they always do.

What about taking the opposite path? What would have happened if I had never talked to that man, the man I had hurt? For the time being, I might have avoided discomfort. But over the course of years, I would have established a hurtful place in my life, a damaged place that could only have grown and grown.

I would have made a lifelong adversary from a potential friend and cut off any possibility of healing.

We can invite a higher power into the process.

Many years ago, I visited the offices of a man of great faith and achievement. I was surprised to see a huge sign on his office wall that read:

> *Lord, there isn't anything that together you and I cannot accomplish today.*

I also remember an extraordinary young woman, not more than 5 feet tall, who took her faith in God very seriously. One Easter Sunday morning, she told me about something that had happened to her on Good Friday. During the worship service, she had had an extraordinary experience. She felt filled with the presence of God in a profound and powerful way.

"I've never had as much of an experience of faith as I did at the service that day," she said. "After the service I went to pick up my sister at the bus terminal. As we walked along 42nd Street, talking, happy to be together, suddenly we were surrounded by five young men who began to taunt us and spit at us."

She said her first reaction had been to be confrontational to meet their aggression with aggression of her own. "But then," she said, "I remembered the faith experience I had just had in church. I began to stand tall, and I looked at the man who seemed to be the leader and said, 'God loves you.' He froze. Again I said, 'God loves you.' He remained still, staring at me. And a third time I said, 'God loves you.' The man began to soften and retreat, and then all five men dispersed."

No matter what trouble faces us, we can always invite God in. Remember the words of God to Joshua. "Be strong. Be courageous. Do not be frightened or dismayed, for the Lord your God is with you wherever you may go."

We can build our courage through openness and take heart.

My father was a minister, a warm, giving, loving, and gregarious man. I think he was an extraordinary pastor. As a little boy, I always liked to be with him when he took walks around our community because that was really where his ministry was. He was more than just the minister of his little Methodist church. He was a beloved man, a minister to the community.

He was born in Italy, and, of course, Italian was his first language. When he stopped to talk to people, he would speak to the older generation in Italian and the younger people in English. But at the end of each conversation, he would shake their hands and say, "Coraggio, coraggio," which is a way of saying, "Courage to you. Stand tall. Walk into the issues of your life today. Don't back off. Take courage." It was like a benediction. "Go with courage. Coraggio."

My father knew that one of the fundamentals of a full life is courage. He knew this because he read the Bible constantly and saw how again and again we are reminded of the extraordinary resources that our faith can provide to deal with any circumstance. When I think of the number of us who just barely touch the surface of what is available, I feel sad. If we would believe and stay with the belief, a very full, complete, wholesome, and happy life is possible.

We can be heartened by tales of other people's courage.

The *Chicken Soup for the Soul* books are full of wonderful, inspirational stories. In *Chicken Soup to Inspire the Body and Soul* (HCI, 2003), one of the books in the series, a man named Dan Millman teaches some valuable lessons about courage. It seems that Dan was complimenting an acquaintance on her courage in facing some very important issues in her life. She replied, "If I have courage, it's inspired by a little boy that I met a long time ago."

She told him how, when she was much younger and volunteering at a local hospital, she had befriended a little girl with a rare disease that was usually fatal. The doctors had tried everything without success. They had one last hope—her 5-year-old brother, who had had the same disease and by some miracle had overcome it, would have antibodies in his blood that might save her life. So the doctor asked the little boy if they could use his blood to help his sister.

After a long pause he agreed. A few days later, as he and his sister lay on adjoining beds, the doctors drew his blood and transferred it to his sister. They watched as life and color came back into her face. Everybody was feeling pretty good.

Then they heard a small voice from the other bed asking, "Doctor, when do I begin to die?" No one had thought to tell the boy he would live through the procedure. He had been willing to give all of his blood so that his sister could live. He believed that he was being asked to die to save his sister, and he agreed anyway. Now, that is bravery.

We can have the courage to admit that we were wrong.

This can be a very big breakthrough. So many of us, after all, cling to the necessity of being right in all situations. We nearly have a fender-bending accident on the way to work, and instead of admitting that we might have been partly responsible, we point at the other driver and say, "That inept idiot was wrong!" Or instead of admitting that we might be contributing to frictions with our spouses or partners or children, we put all the blame on them. We are playing the "right" game: "I am always right, and everyone else is always wrong."

Learning to break free from this cycle can be an important exercise in getting the flow of courage started. Often, courage seems to gain momentum and grow once someone has had the courage to admit wrong and take steps in some new direction.

There are so many other stories of inspiring courage that show that, at the most basic level, courage is doing what must be done simply because we believe it is right. We know what is right, but we have a terribly hard time doing it. Yet if we're going to be worth anything in this human experience, we have to give, and sometimes give it all in taking personal responsibility. When we act knowing it is the right thing to do, we don't have to worry about the return. The return will be waiting for us.

Have you noticed that when you hear stories of courage, they often involve people who are truly surprised to be called "heroes"? It would serve us well, wouldn't it, if people in public places, with high visibility, showed both humility and courage?

It is rare, for instance, that a public figure who has done something wrong clearly and honestly admits the fault and apologizes. It takes courage to say, "I did something wrong. I admit it. I ask you to forgive me."

Maybe you read about something that happened in Boston not long ago. It started with a terrible tragedy. A SWAT team from the police department broke down the door of an apartment on a drug raid. They chased the man who lived there into a back bedroom and handcuffed him. As a result of the shock and rough treatment, he had a heart attack and died.

The police were in the wrong apartment. The man who died was a retired minister who had chosen to stay in the neighborhood to try to bring peace and sanity to a community suffering from an epidemic of violence.

Unfortunately this kind of mistake happens from time to time. But what came next was something we rarely see from a public figure. The Boston police commissioner, Paul Evans, went to the minister's widow and apologized. At the funeral he repeated the apology publicly, taking full responsibility for the behavior of the police, without excuses.

People were stunned. When asked about it, the commissioner said he had made a gut decision, without going to meetings or listening to consultants. He had taken personal responsibility because it was the right thing to do. He went before reporters afterward and simply said that part of being a mature, evolved human being is being able to admit you were wrong. It does not make the pain go away for past actions that were wrong or mean-spirited. But it does represent a vital step in our growth toward becoming mature and responsible human beings.

Part of being a man, or a woman, is saying you're wrong when you're wrong. That belief represents such fundamental honesty and bravery, yet how often do we hear it today?

It's tough to be honest. It takes courage. But we must, even though others might not understand or accept our actions. This is what courage is all about. It's doing what needs to be done because it is right.

Paul Evans was showing a kind of courage that results when we face down our internal fears—the fear of criticism, fear of embarrassment, fear of blame. In a smaller way, I lived the same experience in the days following the boating accident I mentioned earlier in this chapter. When we show the courage to confront such obstacles, we have taken the first step toward overcoming them.

So, in what area might you be dodging issues in just this way? In what area are you sidestepping? In what area are you hiding? What part of your life are you denying because you don't have the courage to stand up and say, "This is what is happening to me," or "This is what I have done"?

Not doing the courageous thing is the same as allowing fear to dominate our lives and actions. Courage is the antidote to fear.

Deepening Our Understanding

As this chapter draws to its end, let me say that there is nothing to be ashamed of in being afraid. Firefighters are afraid. Patients awaiting surgery are afraid. Couples going into counseling are afraid. Alcoholics joining AA are afraid. All the major events and accomplishments in life have their frightening aspects. Fear is with us when we go off to college, get married, or have children. It is facing our fears with courage that makes the difference.

If you feel limited and restricted in your life, unable to reach your fullest potential, perhaps what is missing in you right now, perhaps what could make the difference, is courage. It so often is the difference between the ordinary life and the extraordinary life. The difference between weakness and strength, between living in bondage and being free, and between failure and success is often having the bravery to step out and take responsibility for your life.

13

Freedom Follows Kindness

When I am invited to give a speech, I often suggest a talk on kindness, one of my favorite topics. Yet when I propose it, I sometimes hear objections. People say, "Arthur, a talk about *kindness*? Isn't it superficial? How about something with a little more weight?"

Yet when I speak about kindness, people quickly agree that kindness is a freeing, life-transforming force.

Goethe, certainly no intellectual lightweight, once observed that kindness is not an inconsequential thing—it is a "golden chain" by which society is bound.

Not long ago, a married couple came to see me. They were experiencing extreme difficulty in their marriage. They had become expert at "pushing each other's buttons," and they were constantly fighting. After seeing a counselor for some time, they came back to see me. I was the minister who had married them.

While in my office, they really got into it. They were flinging charges and countercharges at each other. I said, "Quiet, quiet!" but they just continued arguing.

I finally called out, "Please shut up!" I don't often speak that way, but I felt compelled to that time. And even that didn't do any good. In desperation, I actually had to stand between them so they couldn't see one another. This finally embarrassed them enough to stop shouting.

I gave an order: "For one week," I said, "I want each of you to pledge to be kind to the other. If the other says something unkind to you, turn the other cheek. Don't try to defend yourself. Everything you say now is irrational anyway! So you have nothing to lose. I am standing here, ordering you to be kind to each other for a full week."

Now, I don't usually take that kind of tone with people. Most often, I encourage people to find their own solutions. I act as a catalyst. I listen and try not to intrude. But this time, it was clear to me that some stronger measures were required if anything about the marriage could be saved.

After 2 weeks, they came back to see me. They had engaged in some arguments and skirmishes, but somehow their quarrels seemed a little less extreme than before. They both told me that even though they sensed they had a long way to go in mending their relationship, something was beginning to change between them. There was a small light at the end of the tunnel. By simple kindness, they had brought the power of blessing back into their lives. Thanks to kindness, they saw they had a chance. Kindness had freed them to move forward.

What happens when we are not kind in our lives?

- *We drive away the very people we need most—those we love, those upon whom we depend the most.*

- *We poison our own spirits and minds.* Unkindness is like a poison that increases once it is permitted into our system. Small acts and attitudes of unkindness blossom until we end up being unkind people. And we know that unkind people are not *effective* individuals. They become embittered, angry, and immobilized in their lives.

- *We attract only negative, embittered people to travel the road of life with us.* Negativity, we know, attracts more negativity. I believe that you might have shared my experience of encountering groups of people whose entire life experience is predicated on unkindness. They make unkind jokes about unfortunate people. They expect the worst from others, and, as a result, that is just what they receive.

They take joy in the failure of other people. They never forgive. Membership in such poisoned company is certainly not a recipe for personal freedom, healthy decision making, or success.

How can we prevent ourselves from succumbing to the sloppy, self-damaging tendency to be unkind, mean-spirited, and unforgiving in our lives?

We can recall the many acts of kindness that have influenced our life.

As I was gathering my thoughts for this chapter, I began to think of all the acts of kindness that have been done for me during my lifetime. I could have listed a thousand, ten thousand, if I had taken the time.

We can all recall such kind acts. Yet my sense is that most of us do not understand the profound, life-changing impact a simple act of kindness can have on others. I recall something that happened to me on the day my father died. On that day, I was on vacation with my family on a little island off the coast of Maine. Word came from New York that my father had died.

The news quickly spread around the island that Thomas Caliandro had died. Hurriedly, we gathered our things together and packed up so that we could return to New York. As the suitcases were packed, I started placing them outside the back door of our cottage.

Our neighbor from next door, Gail Wood, drove up and began putting our bags into her car. She didn't say a word. I had called a water taxi to shuttle us to the mainland, and Gail drove us down to the boat. It was a simple act of thoughtful, unspoken kindness.

Then 3 weeks later, we returned to the cottage to close it up for the season. We arrived late on a Friday afternoon. There was no food in the house, but Gail soon came walking across the backyard with a big bowl of lobster stew so we would have something to eat that night. I don't even remember what she said, but I remember her simple act of kindness and its profound effect.

We never know the long ripple effect a simple act of kindness can have. But perhaps one way to understand the effect of kindness is to look at it from the other side. Most of us know that a lack of kindness can cut the other way. We're aware of the damage that unkind acts can cause to other people.

Not long ago, on an airplane flight, a fellow passenger, a young woman, was being so unkind to everyone around her that she was having a negative effect on me and all the other passengers. I was one of the first persons on board. I took my assigned seat on the aisle. Soon other people began to file on. This young woman, about 24 years old, appeared. She was well dressed and attractive, but she was in a terrible hurry and impatiently trying to get ahead of the other passengers, so she could get to her seat.

I suddenly became aware that she was going to sit in my row. Before I could get up to let her past me, she kneed her way through me and over me and plopped down in the window seat. She took the blanket and pillow that were there, wrapped herself up, and burrowed in. I thought, "this is going to be interesting."

When the plane was airborne, she leaned over and issued some orders to me: "When they bring the meals, tell them I want one." When the food came, I did that. She woke up. I was there. She was there. It was strange and uncomfortable. She was eagerly eating everything on her plate. I wanted to try to communicate something. Since I wasn't going to eat my dinner roll, I said, "Would you like my roll?"

"No, thank you very much," she answered.

When the plane landed, I stood up and waited for the passengers to file out, as most of us tend to do. But again, she pushed her way right through me. "I want to get out of here," she barked.

She was well dressed and attractive, and she appeared to be bright. I wondered if she was aware of the negative ripple effect her attitude had on so many other people. I am sure she was not aware that, with a simple choice, she could have practiced a small degree of kindness that would have exerted a positive effect on others. And it is such a simple thing to be kind. You can decide that you're going to be kind, and you can be kind. It's that easy.

My experience with that young woman was far different from another experience I had one afternoon in a supermarket. The woman in front of me in the checkout line had three huge bags of oranges. So I said to her, "You must make your own fresh orange juice."

"Yes, I do," she said. "My husband would say to me, 'Honey, if you really love me, you'll give me fresh orange juice every morning.' He's gone now, but I decided I'd continue the tradition. It's a kindness I do to myself."

Isn't that lovely?

Now, where does kindness stand in the great scheme of things? Some of you might say, "You ought to be writing a chapter on something more important than kindness."

I strongly disagree. There isn't anything more important than kindness. In the grand scheme of things, kindness is way up at the top. What would society be like, what would life be like, if everyone were unkind? We would be in a literal living hell.

We can observe all the kindness that surrounds us.

Because I was thinking long and hard about kindness as I worked on this book, I spent a lot of time in New York being very much aware of the kindness I saw around me. In New York, the streets and subways are jammed. We New Yorkers are packed in tighter than sardines in a can. But I noticed incredible civility this week and much, much kindness. I saw deference to the elderly, deference to the disabled, and deference to children.

Oh, yes, perhaps 5 or 6 percent of the people who live here are the other way. They are pushy. But pushiness is not the real spirit of New York City. How many times, over the years, have I seen people stop what they are doing to help strangers who were in trouble or need?

What does Scripture say about kindness? One of my favorite passages on kindness can be found in Matthew, Chapter 25, in the beginning of Verse 31 when Jesus, talking to his disciples, says, in essence:

Remember the time that I was in prison and you came and visited me? Remember the time I was sick and you attended to me? Remember the time I had no clothing and you gave me clothing? And the time I was thirsty and you quenched my thirst? The time I was lonely and you were there for me?

The disciples looked at each other as he was talking. They didn't connect with it.

Then they said, "Lord, we did none of these things for you."

He said, "Oh, yes, you did."

They said, "How?"

Then Jesus said, "Any time you did it to any other human being, you did it to me. Any time you showed respect and caring for another human being, you also did it for me." So the essence of his love is that we must be gentle and kind to one another.

How can we make that happen? As a suggestion, let me point to something that was said by Mother Teresa:

Let's do something beautiful for God.

Those words tell us that even when we disagree with people, even when we are angry, we can do something beautiful for God because we can choose to be kind.

We can take time with each person who comes into our life.

I think we have all seen instances of "selective" kindness. People are kind only to other people who are of their own religion or race, or of their own social class. Or sometimes, they are kind only to people who might have the ability to offer some favors in return.

This kind of kindness is not kindness at all. It is either a way of feeling superior to other people or a bartering system. Neither of those things has anything to do with true kindness.

Some of you will remember Dr. Paul Tournier's name. He was a Swiss psychiatrist and a man of profound spirituality. He wrote with great sensitivity and beauty. In one of his books entitled *The Gift of Feeling* (Westminster John Knox Press, 1988), he talks about a debate he had with one of his colleagues.

This other man said, "What everybody wants more than anything else is to have freedom and equality." Tournier agreed. Those things are indeed important to people. But Tournier added that people also need to be important, to be needed, and to be someone:

> *Take me seriously, even if I don't have a university degree, take me seriously. Even if I'm a laborer, take me seriously. Even if I am black, take me seriously. Even if I am a woman, take me seriously. Even if I'm an immigrant, take me seriously. Even if I have no money, take me seriously. Even if I'm a little child, take me seriously. Recognize me as a person with something valid to say. Take me seriously. I am not a nobody. I am a somebody.*

My freshman year at college was horrendous for me. I was attending college nearly a thousand miles away from my home. I felt insecure and harbored a gnawing fear that I was about to flunk out.

The turnaround began one day during my second semester when my English professor was returning our essay papers to the class. She held mine up. I could see all the red marks and comments on it. I thought, "Oh, what is she going to do? Tear my paper to bits in front of all these other students?"

Instead, she said, "Your grammar and spelling need a lot of work, Arthur, but this is an example of a very well-organized paper."

She had no idea what she had done for me. She had blessed me with an affirmation of kindness. She had told me I could do something well! I knew I could organize thoughts and put them into a sequence. There was a chance for me. Maybe I could make it after all!

As I encountered various setbacks and challenges in college, her small act of kindness helped me press on. Even small acts of affirmation are that powerful. They bring out the best in people and help them bring the full measure of their goodness into the world.

We can commit to taking the high road in all situations.

Kindness frees us to do and act our best in all circumstances. It makes us a little bit stronger and better equipped to meet life's events than we would be otherwise. It puts us in more intimate touch with the world.

It is simple and easy to put these benefits of kindness to work in our lives because every day, life places us in new circumstances where we can make a very simple choice. We can take the high road by thinking and acting kindly or take the low road through unkind acts and thoughts. When you have that kind of choice, it is always wise to make the choice to be kind.

It's a simple way to transform your life and other people's too. In fact, kindness is nearly magical. I have noticed something remarkable about kindness. The moment I have entered the space occupied by a truly kind person, I have felt a wonderful, uplifting influence on my life. I felt as though suddenly, new things were possible for me.

Often, we fall short of being kind for a very shortsighted reason. We have been "stung" before when we made an effort to be kind and other people did not respond. After such experiences, we are tempted to withdraw and become defensive. If we allow that to happen, we cut ourselves off from a closer connection— both to other people and to our spiritual selves.

Several years ago, my wife and I felt the elating force of kindness. We were attending a fund-raising event. We were at the opposite ends of a large room that was filled with people. But even across that hubbub, we exchanged a significant look. My wife knew exactly what was on my mind, and I knew just what was on hers. Separately, we had spotted a woman who projected some extraordinary presence. She was not fashionably dressed, not beautiful. She was simply an older woman with a pleasant face and gray hair. But there was some positive energy in her. She glowed. She was radiant. My wife and I both wanted to get to know her. We worked our way to her side, and we found out that she was everything we thought she might be.

She told us that, during their working years, both she and her husband had been involved in very demanding careers. Now they were retired and were engaged in something unusual. She said that she and her husband, every day, engaged in an activity they called the "Lift Game."

"We simply try to affirm people by being kind," she explained. "Then, when we're having dinner together at the end of the day, we talk about the 'lifts' that we gave to people during the day."

She mentioned an experience she had had the day before. She was making a purchase in a department store. The clerk, a young woman, was sullen and downcast. She said, "I got a glimpse of her teeth and saw they were beautiful. I managed to get her to talk a bit, and then smile. When I saw her give a full smile, I saw how pretty she was, and I told her so. Her smile became broader and she came to life. That is a lift!"

This woman had been a top professional. She had made significant contributions during her working years. Now, she was continuing to make important contributions by excelling in kindness. My wife and I realized we were in the presence of someone who was truly blessed, graced, and extraordinary.

Is that so surprising, really? I don't believe it is. Because when you practice kindness, you are not acting alone. You have become a medium for God's goodwill toward mankind. I'm certain there is not a more significant role to take with your life.

We can strive to empathize.

To empathize means to actually *feel with* another person. It means to strive to experience just what they are experiencing at any given moment or time. Empathy represents an elevated level of kindness.

I know that no one can feel exactly as someone else does at any given moment, especially when that other person is in pain, or acting aggressively, or simply not communicating. Yet even when such obstacles are present, we can still strive to empathize with that other person. The results of simple, kind empathy can be remarkable.

Some years ago, the late Gerd Gunnelfson, my secretary, interrupted a meeting I was conducting at my church. A very distraught man had entered the lobby of the church, asking to see a minister. "I'll go down as soon as I am free," I said, "but if it is really a serious situation, just call and I'll come at once."

After the meeting, I returned to my office and resumed my work. Nearly an hour later, Gerd returned. She had handled the situation on her own. "On the way down," she said, "I tried to get centered within myself and get calm. My idea was to try to carry that calm feeling over into the situation. When I got down there, the man was agitated. I didn't say much. I was simply trying to feel what he felt at the moment, to empathize with him in his emotional state and direct calm feelings his way."

Her silence created an atmosphere that helped him feel safe with himself. She accomplished that without saying many words or asking the man to explain the cause of his alarm. Empathy has that kind of power—to cut through other people's pain silently, as an act of caring kindness.

How many times are we tempted to put people down, to show up their shortcomings, to act in ways calculated to make ourselves feel superior? At such times, we can take the high road. We can be kind. We can slow down the pace of our thinking and judging and listen as those other people speak. Our kindness will lead to empathy and, often, our empathy to deeper understanding. In the end, kindness opens spiritual doors that bring us closer to each other.

Deepening Our Understanding

Cultivating kindness in your own life can be the most powerful of the many steps I recommend in this book. Think small. Get started. Take simple, immediate steps each day that lie within your power. Simply exercise kindness in your next human encounter, sense the good in that act, and keep going. The results will surprise you:

- *Each day will bring you positive new experiences with a widening range of people.* Unkindness shuts the doors of communication to everyone you encounter. Kindness opens those doors. In countless small ways, it opens up new opportunities for cooperation, human contact, and joy.

- *Your positive outlook will soar.* Each kind act and exchange you initiate brings a surge of powerful, positive energy into your life.

Remember that kindness and freedom are closely linked. An unkind life is self-limiting, like a walk down an alley that is ever narrowing and ever darkening. Kindness leads our life in an opposite direction entirely. Each day widens, opening up to bright new vistas of experience and joy.

14

Freedom Follows Forgiving

---

*W*hen we refuse to forgive others, it is like we are agreeing to put on handcuffs. We refuse to forgive one person and cut ourselves off from him or her. With the next person we will not forgive, we cut ourselves off even further. Cumulatively, the damage we do to our lives becomes stifling, and regret, animosity, and sorrow inevitably follow.

But when we learn to forgive actively and with an open heart, new paths immediately open before us. It is as though the dark gray clouds are swept away and we awake into a changed, new day.

Before coming to the Marble Collegiate Church, I served a church in Brooklyn, and in that congregation was an elderly couple I visited often. Finally the day came when we all recognized they could no longer do their own shopping. They agreed that I should find someone. I found a neighbor from across the street who was willing to run errands for them.

Triumphantly I returned. "I found somebody!" But when they heard who it was, there was a visceral reaction. They both backed off.

The husband explained, "Back in 1921, we attended an army reunion dinner from World War I. She and her husband had agreed to sit with us, but when we got there, they were already sitting with somebody else."

The wife chimed in, "And we have never forgiven them."

We are talking about living with a hurt, living with a wrong, for a period of more than 40 years!

A number of years ago I heard a similar story from my barber. "One of my uncles," he told me, "has not seen his son in 15 years. He is still angry at him for not naming his first son after him. Can you imagine that?"

What a tragedy. The man had not seen his son or ever even met his grandson because he would not forgive.

I also remember something that happened one Sunday just after a service in which I had preached a sermon on forgiveness. A woman stopped me and said, "I had great difficulty with your sermon. There are people I just can't and won't forgive!"

She told me about some relatives who, when she was a young girl, had done some very hurtful things to her. As she spoke, her face was contorted. She would not let go of the resentment. Many of us share this problem to a greater or lesser degree, even though we often hesitate to own up to that fact. Or, even worse, we feel that in certain instances we are "right" to refuse to forgive someone. The wrong we suffered at their hands was just too great for us to ever consider forgiving them.

What do we do when somebody has hurt us very deeply and that injury has not only damaged and disrupted our life but has changed us forever? What do we do when the hurt turns into anger, and the anger to resentment, and the resentment buries itself deep into our psyche? That is one of the biggest questions of life. If we are seeking freedom and happiness in life, we need to find a way to let all that hurt go. If we fail to take action to do so, this is what becomes of us:

- *We harbor damaging inner feelings, often for years.* These harmful beliefs and viewpoints never do harm to the people we cannot forgive. They do harm only to us! Failure to forgive, I believe, can become a threat to our personal health. It can become like a small, bubbling cauldron of acid that maintains an inner state of agitation and stress.

- *We cut ourselves off from a growing number of people.* I have one friend who has not spoken to his brother for a period of years. By now his brother has had children my friend has not even seen. Various cousins and aunts and uncles have "sided" with his brother in the dispute, so now my friend never sees those people either! So we see that failure to forgive exerts a negative shock wave in our lives, sweeping people ever further and further away from us.

- *We become rigid, stuck, and unable to move our lives forward.* I have often noticed that rigidity in one area of a person's life quickly infects other areas. First, someone will not forgive a friend or spouse; next, that person will begin to harbor strong, unfounded opinions about what went wrong; and next, that person will begin to harbor foundationless opinions about more and more things. In this way, failing to forgive can act like a kind of mental rigor mortis, spreading into more and more areas of life.

How then can we prevent this damage when learning to forgive can be so difficult?

We can start by recognizing the damage we are doing to ourselves.

The first thing to do is use one of your greatest resources: your mind.

Think. Get a perspective on yourself and what your lack of forgiveness is doing to you. In some quiet moment, try to look with some objectivity at what is going on. You will become aware that all the negative energy welling up within you is detrimental. Study after study has shown a direct correlation between negative emotions and a variety of illnesses. These stresses affect the heart and can even exacerbate certain kinds of cancer. They have been responsible for skin problems and back problems. Just about every disease we have can be affected by negative emotions.

You may be aware of a book written a number of years ago by Norman Cousins called *Anatomy of an Illness* (Bantam Books,

1992). It tells the story of Cousins, who began to feel ill during a whirlwind trip through Russia. He had been "burning the candle at both ends," stressing and pushing himself over the edge. He flew back to America to see his doctor, who told him that he was gravely ill and that he would probably not live much longer. "Norman, you had better get your affairs in order. It's not going to be too long."

How did Cousins respond? He didn't let his emotions carry him away. Instead, he did some thinking, and he realized he had been living too stressful a life. And he reasoned, "If negative emotions can cause illness, then positive emotions can help me get well."

So he designed his own treatment, which involved taking massive doses of vitamin C and watching old *Candid Camera* episodes, which made him laugh and forget his pain and fear. Eventually he got well, and he lived for many more years.

How much is angry resentment negatively affecting the workings of your body? And how much is it affecting your relationships? Only you can answer those questions, and only you can take steps to use forgiveness to let those ill feelings go.

We can strive to understand why we are powerless to forgive.

I do not like to be around people who don't forgive. I don't like feeling their desire for retaliation, their wanting to see the person come to harm. I enjoy being around myself even less when I am locked into that stultifying, immobilizing inability to let go of a past hurt and move on.

I would urge you to consider this, as you look at yourself objectively. Ask yourself two simple questions:

Can I forgive?

If not, why?

If you cannot, you are giving the person who hurt you enormous power and influence over your life. You are actually allowing that unforgiven person to control your mind, your feelings, and your life choices. Even sadder, much of the time the one who injured you has forgotten all about the problems he or she is causing you! He or she is going on with life. You are the one who is controlled by what happened. Do you really want to give that much power to any one person, especially one who has hurt you?

We can get beyond the questions of right and wrong.

There is so much wisdom that tells us that we are never completely right in any conflict or problem:

> *There are more than two sides to every equation. In fact, there are a vast number of possible interpretations and meanings in each. Things are rarely black or white, especially when being considered by many people.*

Of course, this is true. We also know that our own vantage point in any situation or conflict is very much to be distrusted. The words we speak can be interpreted in many ways by the people who hear them, for example. Similarly, the way in which we interpret what we hear is an unreliable gauge by which to assign blame or animosity.

On an even deeper, more pressing level, we need to address our own ego-related needs to be right in the face of life's disagreements and conflicts. So much of the time when we are unable to forgive, we sound exactly like 3-year-old children squabbling with other toddlers:

"He did it first!"

"She has to apologize to me first!"

"I will never admit I was wrong until he does!"

Do we want to live our lives at such an infantile level? Of course, we do not. The first step toward getting past it is often to relinquish the entire issue of right versus wrong in our conflicts.

The point is not that you are right and the other person is wrong. The point is the damage you are doing to yourself by clinging to a limiting, self-damaging conception of a past event.

Only when we elevate our thinking to that higher level can we let go of blame and move our lives ahead.

We can anchor our thinking in examples of the power of forgiving.

Of course, Scripture gives us powerful inspirational teachings on forgiveness. First, in the Gospel According to Matthew, Peter asks Jesus how many times he should forgive, suggesting that seven times might be sufficient. Apparently he had somebody in mind who was giving him a hard time, and he had virtuously counted up the number of times he had forgiven. But Jesus replied:

No, Peter. You must forgive seventy times seven.

Those words tell us that forgiveness is an attitude. Even as you are done harm, you begin the process of forgiving.

We must choose forgiving as an attitude. One first step is to simply think, "I am a forgiving person." That seems simple, but it is surprising how such a simple thought leads us in a new direction in our lives.

Down through history, giants of their times have been forgiving people. Does Abraham Lincoln make sense to you? You know that he does. He was a deeply forgiving man. Does Mahatma Gandhi make sense to you, with his nonviolent leadership? Does Martin Luther King, Jr., make sense?

You may have heard of Corrie ten Boom, a Dutch lady who died in 1983. During World War II, she spent some years in a concentration camp. Then after the war, she traveled to every corner of Europe, preaching and speaking and doing everything she could to bring about healing between former enemies. One night when she was speaking at a church in Germany, a man approached her to compliment her on her talk.

She recognized him as a man she had hated. He had been among those responsible for the death of her sister in the concentration camp. In that instant, Corrie ten Boom was able to find the strength to forgive him. And in that moment, she freed herself. What a superhuman effort! Could you make such an effort, such a decision? Could I? In honesty, I could not tell you for certain. Yet her example calls upon us to think, to ponder the issue of forgiveness at the highest level. Does Corrie ten Boom make sense? What does her example, of forgiving a true enemy who tried to destroy her, and who did destroy her sister and so much else, tell us about the path we could choose to pursue in our lives?

Did it make sense the last time you forgave somebody? Do you remember the freedom you felt, how released and clean you felt inside? You know that made sense.

We can be prepared for the hard work of forgiving.

Now, getting to the point of forgiveness doesn't come easily. It isn't like taking a cloth and wiping off a blackboard. It takes work, prayer, pain, and patience. But if diligently you seek to forgive, if you diligently pray for help in forgiving, in time it's going to happen. And what a difference it makes.

Some time ago, I read an article that described the approaches that former president Jimmy Carter and his wife Rosalynn had used to keep their marriage happy and secure over a period of more than 50 years.

He observed that along the way, he and his wife Rosalynn had had difficult times and plenty of arguments, yet they had learned to forgive each other. I remember that he described an argument that had gone on for days, in which he and his wife could hardly even speak to each other.

Finally, he went to his woodworking shop and fashioned a facsimile of a printed bank check from a piece of walnut. On it, he wrote that it served as an apology or forgiveness, which ever was needed, good for the rest of their lives. Then he signed it and gave it to Rosalynn.

Often in wedding ceremonies, when I'm asked to say something beyond what is written on the page of the standard ceremonial words, I talk about forgiveness. I tell the couple they must learn to forgive and forgive and forgive. I say that without forgiveness, the relationship will eventually wither and die. With forgiveness, everything is possible.

We can learn to question our own point of view.

In his book *Seven Habits of Highly Effective People* (Simon & Schuster, 1990), Stephen Covey writes about an experience he had on a subway train one Sunday morning. The car was full of people. Some people were reading the paper, some were in thought, and some were resting with eyes closed. Into this calm and serene car came a man with two children. The man sat next to Stephen Covey and then slumped down with his eyes closed, while his children proceeded to run all around the car, out of control. They were throwing things, making noise, and bumping up against people who were trying to read their papers. Mr. Covey found himself increasingly annoyed and irritated and finally said, with as much restraint and patience as he could, "Sir, would you mind trying to control your children? They're bothering people."

The man shook himself. "Yes, yes, I guess I should do that. . . . We just came from the hospital. Their mother died an hour ago. . . . I don't know how to handle it, and neither do the kids."

How many times have you and I been in situations like that? We didn't ask questions, we didn't take time to figure out what was going on, and we didn't try to get behind the behavior. We made no effort to understand what was motivating the behavior or problem we were troubled by, and we made our judgments and later felt badly about doing so?

I remember as a boy seeing on a classroom wall a Native American saying: "I must walk twelve moons in a man's shoes before I can judge him." And I think of something that Henry Wadsworth Longfellow said, that if we knew the secret history of our enemies, they would no longer be our enemies.

The great religious traditions, in their own way, teach this fundamental principle:

> *Judge not, that you be not judged. Condemn not, that you be not condemned. Seek to love, empathize and affirm, and good things will come back to you.*

We can practice the art of forgiveness.

I have often found it hard to forgive. I've been seduced by the tendency to blame at various times in my life. Like many people, I have found it easier to point a finger of blame at someone else instead of taking responsibility for solving problems myself.

After all, "It's her fault" or "It's his fault" represent very seductive ways to explain our own shortcomings. Yet freedom lies in our power, when we are injured, to begin the process of forgiving. I know that this is not easy advice to follow, but I urge you to begin the process of forgiving anyway.

I would like to share with you a lesson from the Talmud, which is related by Dr. Doris Donnelly in her wonderful book *Learning to Forgive* (Macmillan, 1979). According to one law of the Talmud, if you are given the choice of first helping a friend or helping an enemy, you should first help the enemy! Why? Because when you help an enemy first, you destroy first the hostile emotions and hatred in the enemy and then those emotions in yourself. Instead of an enemy, you have a friend and ally.

Here is a simple process that can help you get started in your quest to forgive and experience the letting-go of emotions that can only be detrimental to you:

- *Pray for the person you want to forgive.* We know the words "Love your neighbor . . . pray for the person who tries to harm you." Pray for the people who have harmed you? What negative feelings this step can conjure up! Yet it can be an essential first step in the forgiveness process. Try it. It is powerful and liberating.

- *Take responsibility for the harm the "unforgivable" person has caused.* This is another difficult step, to be sure! After all, pride is the greatest obstacle to forgiveness. In many instances where we direct blame at another person, we are simply looking for an "out" that lets us divert blame from ourselves. If we can set aside that pride and blame ourselves, we discover the very tools we need to do even better in the future. We empower ourselves to learn by saying, "Here's the mistake I made, and here's how I can avoid making it a second time."

- *Actively forgive the person you blame.* Here is another opportunity to create a dividing line between today and the past. Even if you are having a difficult time forgiving someone who is no longer alive, you can simply conjure up an image of that person and say, "I forgive you." The results of this simple step can be surprisingly emotional and liberating. An emotional burden lifts from your shoulders. You can live better, today.

- *Apologize to the people you have harmed.* During the Jewish high holy days, on the Day of Atonement (Yom Kippur), worshipers are asked to actually speak to the people whom they have harmed in the last year. They are supposed to go to those people and address them directly, saying, "This is what I did to you. I ask you to forgive me." How many of us could do that? What difficult advice it is to follow! Yet consider the tremendous release we can initiate when we apologize, admitting our wrong in the blame-causing situation in which we are caught. It can be the first step toward learning the process of forgiving—a process that can transform our lives.

Deepening Our Understanding

I would be telling a mistruth if I said that forgiveness is easy. It isn't! It can be one of the most difficult things we could ever demand of ourselves.

Yet what rich rewards await us when we do the hard work and learn to forgive:

- *We release negative feelings that we've bottled up inside—often for a period of months or years.* Stress and inner turmoil release, leaving us full of new energy to do better in all our human relationships.

- *We reconnect with people on a deeper, often spiritual level.* Blame is like a screen that comes between us, blocking our full view of how wonderful people can be and the positive force they can exert over our lives.

- *We become energized and better able to move our lives forward.* Areas that were closed, blocked off by blame, are suddenly open to us.

Our first glimpse of new freedom follows just as soon as we decide to begin the hard work of getting blame out of our lives.

15

Freedom Follows
Thinking about the Hereafter

*L*et me stress at the outset that, in this chapter, I will not be asking you to believe in life after death. That is not my open purpose for this chapter, nor is it my hidden agenda for you. If you do not believe in life after death, there is nothing I can tell you in this chapter that could convince you to believe otherwise. Conversely, if you do believe in life after death, there is nothing I could tell you in one short chapter that could change your point of view.

I am simply asking you to *think* about the question of whether you will go on to other things after your time on earth is over. I am asking you to trust me when I ask you to begin this inquiry because I have seen the difference it has made in so many people's lives. Some have come away with new beliefs and new convictions, others have not. But all of them have achieved a more informed perspective on where they are with their lives, and where they might go if they stayed oriented toward the larger questions of living.

In one sense, I cannot prove it to you. But in another sense, I can.

Remember that I am speaking from the perspective of my own faith experience, only one man's story. We learn and grow from hearing each other's stories. I cannot say that I expect you will agree with everything I have to tell you. I only hope you will find my comments and views useful.

First, we need to remember that we are all works in progress. There is movement in our lives, a living and growing dynamic. We are ever stretching and absorbing new ideas.

When I contemplate the possibility of life after death, I am made aware of how much mystery there is in our life experience. There is so much we don't know, so much that is really unknowable.

Consider the fact that birth is a mystery. We don't know why we are born at the time we are, to the parents we are, nor where we come from. Birth is a mystery as great as death might ever be, yet none of us doubts its existence.

Our feelings are a mystery too. Why are we drawn to certain circumstances and people? Why do we experience such curious mixtures of love, hate, sorrow, and happiness? What is this confusion of feelings inside of us? What a great mystery they are!

God is certainly a mystery. So many of us try to understand and experience some higher presence in our lives, but we never fully understand or grasp what it is or how it operates. We can only make attempts to fathom it. God is one of the greatest mysteries of all, yet most of us believe that this greater power is present in our lives.

Death is another mystery. We know it's going to happen. We don't know how or when, what the circumstances will be.

And as great a mystery is life after death. Does life continue?

We know we are going to die, yet most of us don't want our lives to end. Built into us at birth, at our very center, the core of our psyches, is the spark of life itself. There is in each one of us the spark of the divine, and in that spark, there seems to be a desire for life never to stop.

What happens to us when we refuse to even admit the possibility of life after death? I modestly admit that I do not understand all the ramifications that can affect a person who has shut off the issue from further exploration and thought. But here are some negative effects that I have noticed time and time again:

- *We no longer care so deeply about the future of the world.*
  What about the environment? What about the future of
  humanity, or of our children? With no investment in
  some eternal life, such considerations lose their immense
  importance.

- *We cling to life in obsessive, often unhealthy ways.* Part of
  living graciously and well, I believe, is our willingness to
  cede our place on this earth to the next generation. We
  have had our time here, our rightful leg on this part of
  our spiritual journey. A belief that we will now be moving
  on in an appropriate way helps us not cling to life here in
  a hopeless, tragic way.

- *We rob our lives of an important spiritual dimension.* We're
  only here, moving from Point A to Point B. We have only
  so many years, just so many steps we can take. A belief in
  the hereafter, by necessity, pushes back those borders of
  our self-conception. We become bigger, embodying an
  eternal aspect. This bigger view of ourselves can only
  make our time here on earth more complete, more
  rewarding, more free, and more inspiring.

How can we begin this search—not the search for belief in
life after death but for a bigger self-conception that results from
seeing ourselves as part of an eternity, not a finality?

We can begin to entertain the question.

Just entertain it! That sounds simple, yet it can be a challenging
step in its own right.

For many years I doubted the existence of life after death.
Does life really continue after we die? How could that possibly
be? I didn't want to doubt it, but I couldn't help myself. I strug-
gled long and hard, wanting to believe that life would continue.
But the truth is that I just couldn't, which is surely a difficult
thing for a member of the clergy to admit. As you all are aware,

willpower has little power to make one change. Change comes not from the head but from the heart.

An illustration of how completely I questioned the idea of life after death was my reaction to an incident that occurred in my senior year of seminary. The school had a practice of asking clergy parents of students to preach at a chapel service. My father, a Methodist minister, was invited to preach.

He was thrilled to have been asked, as he often felt shy and inferior. He was sensitive about his thick Italian accent. He felt that his education was lacking. He was serving a very small church in Queens. He felt honored, and he was eager to do a good job.

My doubts about life after death ruined whatever joy my father might have experienced that proud day. In his sermon, he told a story about a man who, standing in his bedroom one day, was startled by a sudden gust of wind that blew through the open window and knocked a picture of his own father off the dresser. He sensed immediately that his father, who lived far away, had died. Moments later, the telephone rang with the news that he had been right. His father had indeed passed on.

I had trouble with that story, although I don't have trouble with it now. Since that day, I have heard about too many "coincidences" where the soul appears to communicate with loved ones as it leaves this life.

I wonder if that happened to me recently. My wife and I were in the British West Indies. Early one morning I took a long walk, and for most of the journey, a butterfly flew along in front of me, flittering about this way and that. In all the years I've been taking morning walks, never had I seen a butterfly stay with me the whole way. I wondered! A very dear friend had died a few days before. Could this have been her way of telling me, "Arthur, it's okay. I'm free"?

But on the day my father spoke, I had not had such experiences, or at least I was not owning up to them. After that chapel service as my father and I greeted the minister, I saw the spark in my dad's eye, indicating he was feeling good about his sermon. I would like to take back what I said to him then. "Daddy," I said, "why did you use that illustration about the man dying and making the picture fall down?" In that instant I saw the joy leave him.

We can open our eyes to remarkable events that often accompany the time when people leave this world.

A friend of mine tells me that on the night his mother died, a clock stopped, a mirror fell from a wall, and he heard a loud pounding in the ceiling over his bed! Yet even at that, he wrote it all off and, for many years, refused to even consider the possibility that as his mother left this world, some kind of spiritual energy was at work, causing disruptions in the world his mother was leaving behind.

If you look at your own family history, I would be willing to predict that you will find similar stories too. You, or those around you, may have written them off as superstitious, "old country," not worthy of your modern mind. Yet such events are so commonplace that I'd urge you to bring them up to the top of your mind and explore them in the objective light of day.

After all, there is a very thin veil between this life and the life beyond, between mortality and immortality, earth and heaven. This was illustrated dramatically for me on the day my father died. All of his children and grandchildren, except for my older brother, happened to be on a little island off the Maine coast. At eleven o'clock that morning, an alarm sounded at the island's fire station and volunteer firefighters raced to their posts on the engine. Then my sister-in-law, my older brother's wife, did something that seemed completely uncharacteristic of her. She got in her station wagon, gathered up the entire family, and followed the fire engine as it rushed to the other end of the island. But there was no fire. Nobody knew who called in the signal.

An hour later, my older brother called from New York to tell us that our father had died. I realized the connection between the two events only some days later. At the same time my father was passing through the thin veil into the next life, he did something to gather all his family together. Could it have been his way of saying to me, "Arthur, what I preached in the seminary was right. You need to pay attention to this question of whether the soul goes on. This kind of thing does happen."

Again I believe there is a very thin veil between this side and the other.

We can listen to the advice of experts and researchers in the area.

When we are researching arthritis, or healthy food, or most other topics, we are always happy to consider the findings and beliefs of experts in the field. Why is it, then, that we often resist considering the findings of people who have investigated the possibility of life after death? There is much evidence that life continues—evidence not only of faith, but also of fact.

You may be familiar with Dr. Elisabeth Kübler-Ross, the psychiatrist from Switzerland who immigrated to America and has written the definitive work on death and dying. She has spent thousands of hours with dying patients researching the experience of dying. We were privileged to have her lecture at my church several years ago. During that evening I said to her, "I believe I heard that when you began your work, you were an atheist and didn't believe in life after death."

"That's right," she said. "I didn't."

She told me that in the time she had spent with dying people, she had discovered something transcendent. In the midst of death there was so much life. And she talked about people who had been considered clinically dead but had been resuscitated and had reported their experience of life on another plane. She began to see and believe that life does not end with death. Life continues.

In the end, she concluded that the experience of dying is very much like the experience of being born. Like birth, dying is a natural and human process. As a scientist, she concluded that in both birth and death we are never alone.

I am guided by this philosophy. I believe that when we die, our starting point on the other side, just beyond the veil, is where we leave off here. I believe the soul travels a path of continuous growth. So when I die, I want to be as far along the path in emotional, mental, and spiritual health as I can be.

Sometimes people who are in their final years ask me why they should work so hard to grow spiritually. Since there is so little time left, they feel there is little reason to keep growing, particularly since growth can require a faith and strength of spirit that is hard to come by. My response is based on my philosophy. I urge them to continue growing, knowing that nothing is wasted and that their souls will benefit after they have passed on to the other side.

The much-respected preacher and writer, the late Leslie Weatherhead, offers his perspective on life after death in the book *Time for God* (Abingdon Press, 1967):

> *In my view this life is the lowest form in God's school. . . . Death is only passing into another form in God's school, but it would be wise, especially in the second half of life, to prepare for it. We shall put down the body with all its lusts and desires. Money and possessions, social status, and academic distinction are all left behind.*

Each of us is a work in progress. Just on the other side of a very thin veil are our angels, our guardians, and those who have passed on before us. They are with us now and will greet us when we die into the next level.

Deepening Our Understanding

To have a full, active, and productive life, we do not need to believe in life after death. Yet it is such a major issue, one that has been contemplated by many of the greatest minds of the ages, that I believe it is a mistake to simply "write it off" and think about it no more.

By approaching the issue, we propel ourselves toward bigger issues:

- Why am I here?

- Am I leaving an imprint of my life that will be remembered?

- How do I want to be remembered?

- What is my legacy to those who will live after me, and why is that important?

- What is my contribution to the world at large?

- What is my legacy to this world?

- Is there an infinite aspect to my life, something that will go on forever?

- What has really become of the people I have known and loved in the past who are no longer with me?

- Is there something about my soul that might continue onward after my body is no longer alive?

Tough questions to ask! They represent an open invitation to a long and self-testing path of inquiry. But at the end lies a bigger understanding of life—its freedoms, limitations, boundaries, and joys.

I believe the insight, made famous by Teilhard de Chardin, that we are souls first and foremost. We come from a spiritual place and go back to a spiritual place. The purpose of life is growth in that spiritual dimension.

16

Freedom Follows
Letting Go of Prejudice

*O*n hearing the word *love*, we generally think of romantic love—sweet, sentimental, and tender. Romantic love is amazing. And because humans are beings that need and desire love, we usually give romantic love our all, our very best.

When we are in love, we see the best in those we love. We notice everything about them, and we listen with deep interest when they speak.

What would it be like if we could bring that same tender, caring regard to all our relationships? We require love, attention, and acceptance from the people around us, and everyone we meet does too.

How wonderful it would be if we could all free ourselves from prejudice! How much more wonderful our lives would be. How much more wonderful the world would be too.

Yet instead of accepting people equally and seeing them for who they really are—kindred souls who are sharing our experience on this earthly journey—we seem driven to place obstacles between ourselves and everyone else:

- "I accept everyone equally, as long as they don't try to marry my son or daughter, as long as they remain where they belong," I heard a man say. When we think this way, we are lying to ourselves. We cannot be open and closed, prejudiced and accepting. There is no fence-sitting in this critical area of life, no vacillating.

- "I have no prejudices against gay people, and I work with several gay men, but I will make jokes about them when they are not around," another man told a group of friends recently. No prejudices, yet he will tell jokes about homosexuals behind their backs? He pretends to operate on a fair, even field with gay people, yet makes fun of them. If people can accept such double standards in one area of their lives, I am willing to wager that they will accept them in other areas too.

- "In the wake of the attacks on the World Trade Center, I have come to see Islam as a religion of hate," a woman told me lately. Yet when we discussed this viewpoint at length, it became clear to me that she knew almost nothing about Islam or its practitioners. Because of the actions of a small, insulated minority of Muslims, she was willing to make a quantum leap in her prejudice and condemn all the practitioners of one of the great religions of the world.

Prejudice is a tempter and a temptress. It starts with patterns of thinking that appear to us to be logical. But once we give in to the temptation and allow it to infect us, it can distort and damage our view of the world. Once it gains a foothold in our lives, its potential to harm us is extreme:

- *We begin to feel superior to others.* "They" do things wrong. "They" don't live in ways, in places, that we deem appropriate. "They" don't impart the right values to their children. "They" practice faiths that are incorrect, that will not qualify them for the full bounty of God's grace. "They" are sinners because of their sexual orientation. "They" are cheap, or stupid, or sneaky. "They, they, they . . ." Such false posturing of superiority desperately damages the world view of the person who succumbs to it.

- *We draw boundaries that put us at risk.* In my book *Simple Steps*, I related the story of a man whose father always disliked Hispanic people until he was in an automobile accident and was rescued by a Hispanic man. How many times in that man's life had he cut himself off from sources of good before that car accident occurred? How many times did he cut himself off from help, goodwill, good ideas, and good friendship? There is no reason to incur this kind of damage from prejudice. We can decide to rid our lives of it.

- *We begin to think irrationally and limit ourselves.* "I will never speak to my grandson because he married someone of another faith," I heard a woman say last year. Never speak to her grandson? Never get to know her great-grandchildren, never learn about the woman her grandson chose to be his wife? How limiting, how senseless is such discrimination in our lives.

- *We use stereotypes to condemn people.* We all know them by heart—the stuff of unkind jokes, snide remarks, and outright prejudice. They are not fair to the people who are targeted, to our society—and ultimately, not to ourselves.

- *We do damage to the world.* History tells us that the world is a place where all human advancement and growth has taken place not through war and animosity but rather through the ability of people to understand each other and draw closer. It would not be an exaggeration to say that when we are prejudiced, when we do not take part in that process, we are inhibiting the chances that the world will one day be peaceful and free of hatred and war.

In light of all this damage prejudice inflicts on us and on our world, how can we turn the situation around? How can we rid ourselves of this insidious, damaging harm? I might mention that it is an especially pressing problem to consider in the current time of war in Iraq, when prejudice against our enemies—or former enemies—can become especially widespread. I grew up after

World War II, when hatred of Japanese Americans was especially widespread, and especially wrong. We need to guard against such irrational prejudices against Arab Americans today.

We can be a powerful force of love.

You may not feel a passion for other people, but the ability to do so is in you. What would it be like if tomorrow morning you left your house committed to loving everybody with a deep interest, a genuine passion? You would walk out the door and feel an active affection for whomever you met—your neighbor, your doorman, the bus driver, the postal carrier.

When you got to your place of work, even with all the problems you might encounter, you would decide that you were going to have a loving feeling for everybody, no matter what. No matter how people reacted to you, no matter how irritating they might be, you're going to be loving to them.

Perhaps you are looking for a job tomorrow, going on a job interview. What would happen if you were to be loving to the people interviewing you? Suppose when you walked through the door, you didn't see a white person or a black person or a Latino person or an Arab person or a gay person but just another human being. Someone worthy of the right to earn your respect and affection, not someone to be dismissed. You might be surprised by how well your interview goes.

If you try this, you might say to me, "I loved people for a whole day. When I got home, I was exhausted. Besides, you should have seen how surprised people were."

Perhaps for a few days you *will* feel exhausted. Other people who have encountered you may, in contrast, feel exhilarated and might look at you strangely. But after a while this will pass, and you will find that you are energized. That is because, through your loving behavior, you will have established a new climate, an emotional, mental, spiritual climate, conducive to helping and building. You will find that the world will begin to respond to you in a very different way. You will prove the old saying "Love the world and the world will love you back." And you will have struck a blow against prejudice—your own and the world's too.

We can pray for the person or persons toward whom we feel prejudice.

This is a truly powerful step toward eliminating prejudice in our lives and our hearts. When we pray for the people we are inclined to dislike, we feel our hearts moving in the direction of greater acceptance and greater love.

In only a short time, we can feel ourselves changed by the force of acceptance as it replaces distrust and hate.

We can remind ourselves to see people as individuals, not members of groups.

I had just conducted a funeral at a church in Brooklyn. Carrying my prayer book and robe, I was walking toward my car. It was midday, and I felt safe. But suddenly I was stopped by three teenage boys. One of them held a knife to my stomach while the others robbed me.

If you have had such an encounter, you know how it feels. And you also know the lingering effects, how that fear hangs on. For months afterward, any time I saw teenage boys about the age of my assailants, and of the same background, and dressed about the same, I had a visceral reaction. They were my enemy even though I didn't know them. The demon prejudice was at work in me, no question about it.

I had to take charge of my reaction and work it through, telling myself that not all teenagers who looked like my attackers were dangerous. Otherwise, I would have allowed my whole internal system to build up a rigid resistance to people I didn't even know.

I also remember that when I was a college freshman, I experienced for the first time what it is like to be on the other side of prejudice, as a victim. A few weeks before the Christmas holiday,

I started dating a young woman I liked. After vacation, excited about seeing her again, I called her for a date. But she very abruptly told me that she could not see or speak to me anymore. I was devastated.

Unable to learn from her why she rejected me, I sought the answer from her roommate. She told me that the parents of the girl I had been dating had found out that I am of Italian heritage, and they had forbidden her to date me or even to speak to me. I remember thinking that they disliked me without even knowing me. That was very painful to me.

We can remember that we are all souls on an earthly journey.

The Scriptures tell us a great deal about prejudice. One is a story about a Jewish man who was accosted, beaten up, robbed, and left by the side of the road to die.

Three people passed by. The first two were officials of a temple, considered to be upstanding citizens. But each chose not to stop and help. The third man did stop. He took his time. He spent his money. He gave the best of himself.

That man was a Samaritan. In those days, the Jewish people and the Samaritan people were prejudiced against each other. According to Jewish opinion, any Samaritan was a bad person and not to be trusted. But the Samaritan put aside prejudice and helped his Jewish neighbor.

It is human frailty to see faults in others, but are we as willing to examine ourselves for those same faults? Sometimes the flaws we see so clearly in others are precisely those flaws we ourselves possess.

We can commit ourselves to a higher process.

Where prejudice is at issue, many people among us take the wide and easy road—the low road, built for the lowest common denominator. Very few people choose the high and narrow road.

What do I mean, a high and narrow road?

Simply that when you climb a mountain, at the bottom the road is wide and easy. As you climb, the road narrows and becomes more difficult. But once you make this hard climb, you can see the magnificent panorama of life around you. In the same way, when you take the narrow road in life, you reach the high place. You have a broader view of the life experience.

Similarly, when we are tempted by the demon of prejudice, small-mindedness, and meanness, we can decide to stand tall on the inside. When we hear other people making jokes at the expense of "other" people, we can speak up and say that such jokes are not appropriate. When we hear words or see deeds that marginalize or hurt people, we can speak up.

It is not an easy path to follow, but we can actively seek to be bigger than prejudice. Bigger than our own prejudice, and even bigger than the prejudice of the world.

Inside you is enormous love. You know it's there. Make the right decision and allow it to happen.

We can be careful not to draw the line anywhere.

As I mentioned earlier in this chapter, part of the evil of prejudice is that it seduces us into thinking that there are times when it is acceptable. We are still "good" people even though we feel it is permissible to dislike black people, or Pakistani people, or gay people, or members of some discrete group.

It is vital to resist this thinking. It is a subterfuge that allows us to accept that thinking illogically is logical some of the time, that thinking maliciously is permissible some of the time. It is a kind of thinking that makes no sense and does us damage.

Deepening Our Understanding

Don't get caught in the prejudice trap. Get to know people. Let yourself love people. And always give others the chance to earn your love or even your dislike. Let it be based on that individual person, not the "group" where you place them because of your own beliefs, prejudices, or experiences.

If we can break prejudice's hold on our lives, many extraordinary benefits will accrue:

- *We will be woven into the wonderful richness of the full human family.* With acceptance and love in your heart, you will see what each person is really like. With your heart and mind opened to what all people bring, your life will be opened to welcome in all the riches they bring to you.

- *We build a better world.* History tells us that the world was not made better by armies, by crusaders, or by wars. The world was made better, one person at a time, by individuals who were able to direct focused, extraordinary love at the brothers and sisters they met in the process of living.

- *We gain new control and freedom over our lives.* Each person's ideas become welcome to us. Each person we meet becomes a possible partner in life's journey.

How much richer and freer our lives become when we turn to face our prejudices, stare them down and say in word and deed, "There is no longer any place for you in my life."

A new way of living can open before us, a new path toward freedom and happiness. It all starts with taking even a few small steps away from antipathy toward love.

17

Freedom Follows
Taking the Higher Road

*T*ake the higher road!" You will find those words in other
places in this book. Even when I have not used those words
exactly, the principle of taking the higher path in life is one that
we have touched upon often.

We are offered many choices each day when the easier, more
convenient choice is to take a lower road that lies before us. We
can be harsh instead of kind and loving. We can hold grudges, or
we can forgive. We can conceal the fact that we are wrong, or we
can admit it and do what we need to do to make things right. We
can harbor negative outlooks or a positive attitude. We can be
open to all people, or we can cling to prejudice.

The choice is ours. Simple as the concept seems, our choice
to take the higher road lies at the very center of many of the daily
choices we make as we determine the trajectory of our lives.

Which way should *you* go? Up or down? It is a simple choice,
yet it is one that can make all the difference in the quality of the
life you have chosen to lead. Few decisions will influence you as
profoundly.

I remember a summer night when I was reading in the study
of my little cottage in Maine. Suddenly, someone rapped on the
window! It was a young man, a neighbor, who looked as if he
were carrying the weight of the world on his shoulders.

"Arthur, can we talk?" he asked. "I hope you won't be angry
with me, but I need to tell you something. Do you remember

when you had a well drilled on your property, soon after you moved here?"

I certainly did. Twenty years before, we had had a new well drilled. It was late summer. I had the drilling done before the winter so that I could have the pump and other hardware installed the following spring.

But winter came and went, and when a contractor came to complete the work, he found the hole completely blocked. He couldn't even drop a thin plumb line down to where the water was! It was sealed, rock solid. He thought perhaps the winter frost had caused the casing to shift, shutting it off. So we called back the well-driller, who suggested the real problem was vandalism. He told us that he strongly suspected that someone had thrown rocks down the shaft and blocked it intentionally.

After much expense and many weeks of hassling, including bringing heavy equipment back to the island and redrilling the well, we finally got our water. But I never knew the real cause of the problem until that summer night when that young man sat in my study and told me that he had thrown rocks down the well and jammed it intentionally. I did not ask why. It may have been an impulse that sprang from dislike of me or simple adolescent meanness. I did not need to know.

"Will you forgive me?" he asked.

"Yes, I forgive you," I said. And then I added, "It must have taken enormous courage for you to come here."

"It wasn't courage. I had to tell you. Every time I saw you, I felt guilty."

I was deeply moved.

"I'd like to make restitution," he told me.

I said, "No, that's not necessary. Instead, when you have an opportunity to help somebody, use the money to help."

We shook hands and parted friends. It was important that he confessed. He needed to do it, and I needed it as well. And he did the right thing. He took the higher road. His confession was healing for both him and me. What bravery it took!

That incident is a simple, true example of the transforming power of taking the higher road. It is a choice we are called upon to make many times every day. In every encounter with other people, we can be either kind or heartless. In every situation, we can be forgiving or inflexible. We can be polite or brusque. We can make the time to listen to other people, or we can cut them off and dismiss them. We can be flexible and dependable with our loved ones, or harsh and rigid.

We have many choices to make every day throughout our lives. And when we take the lower road, we do ourselves irreparable harm in countless ways:

- *We become opinionated and limited in our outlook.* We dismiss the views of others and cling only to our own ways. This is a prescription for a limited life with a limited perspective.

- *We accumulate regrets and remorse.* Often, we are unkindest to the people who share our lives most intimately. If this pattern is allowed to go on for years, we do irreparable harm to our loved ones and closest friends.

- *We become unattractive, unappealing, and finally, unloved.* No one likes to spend time in the company of someone who has become embittered, biased, dogmatic, and dismissive of other people's ideas. And that is just what we become when we consistently direct our steps toward the lowest, rather than the highest, course of action.

- *We lose the perspective we need to make the right decisions and take the best actions in our lives.* Taking the lower road cripples us. In practical terms, a string of poor decisions will inevitably move our lives into a downward cycle of negativism.

How then can we orient our lives in the right way? How can we gain the courage and perspective to consistently direct our steps toward the higher path?

We can consistently seek to take the higher road.

The first step is to become consciously aware that the higher road is an option that is always available to us. It is always there, no matter the situation we are confronting.

We can consistently remind ourselves, "Do the right thing; seek the higher road." This awareness is the first step along this new life path.

We can anticipate, even welcome, the difficulty of the process.

Doing the right thing rarely is easy! In seeking it, and taking it, you have to be aware that you may be criticized, judged, or even ostracized.

"You're foolish!" people will tell you. "You don't have to be so honest, so kind, so caring."

It is often difficult to make the decision to take the higher road. But, as a friend of mine says, anybody who does that consistently ends up "on the side of the gods."

We can be flexible, consistently seeking to identify and understand what taking the higher road might entail.

Sometimes life issues are clear, but more often they are confusing. After all, we do not live in a black-and-white world.

A number of years ago a professor at Harvard Divinity School, Joseph Fletcher, wrote a controversial book called *Situation Ethics* (Westminster John Knox Press, 1966).

Each situation, he argued, deserves a thoughtful look. He suggested that love and compassion often transcend accepted rules. He also urged his readers to cultivate "free and innovative thinking" in opposition to rigid adherence.

As an example of this principle, he reported an encounter that one of his friends had experienced with a taxi driver. It occurred as a presidential campaign was drawing to its conclusion. The man and the driver began talking politics and discovered they were both Republicans. "You must be voting for Senator so-and-so," said Fletcher's friend.

"No, I'm not," replied the taxi driver.

This surprised his passenger. "Why not?" he asked.

"Sometimes, you have to push principle aside and do the right thing," the driver responded.

I think we have all faced similar situations when what we feel to be the right thing must take precedence over our usual path. Strictly following the rules and principles that normally guide our lives may not yield a fair or compassionate result. Flexibility is required.

A good example of this occurred several years ago. The excellent University of Connecticut women's basketball team was approaching the end of a season. One of their star players, Nykesha Sales, was about to break the school's all-time scoring record. A great player! She had just one point to go when she injured her Achilles tendon and had to be carried off the playing floor.

It was certain she would have broken the record in that game or surely in the next. It was a shame she would have to miss such a golden moment! Then her coach had an idea. He called the coach of Villanova, their next opponent, and enlisted his cooperation in allowing Nykesha an uncontested shot so she could break the record.

At the beginning of the game, Nykesha, with her leg brace and crutches, made the shot and broke the record. Although many people were glad for this compromise, others were critical.

Villanova fans objected, "You're breaking the rules! You're setting a bad precedent!"

But Dave Anderson, sports writer for the *New York Times,* wrote an article about it that was like a short treatise on the benefits of taking a higher road when it is available. He concluded by saying, "Yes, it was wrong. But it was a nice wrong."

We can follow the Golden Rule.

During my freshman year in college, a fellow student and friend of mine boasted that he had an extra $10 because a dry cleaner had given him the wrong change. When I looked questioningly at him, he responded, "Arthur, you've got to understand that when you go into business, you take a risk! Some days you lose and some days you win. Today they lost, and I won."

His attitude and response bothered me. He was not living by the Golden Rule. The Golden Rule is truly the wisdom of the ages, encapsulated in a few short words:

Do unto others as you would have others do unto you.

From a situational perspective, the Golden Rule means that you pledge to respect every other human being, just as you want that person to respect you. You care about every other human being as you would want every other human being to care about you.

The value of living the rule can be discovered suddenly, at surprising moments in our lives. Not long ago, I was talking with a young man, a tough and very combative soul, who had recently been in an altercation that came to blows. "Arthur, I was surprised at myself," he said. "When he hit me, I didn't hit him back. For some reason I stood there and I let him hit me."

Seeing that he was getting no response, the aggressor had dropped his arms. He looked ashamed and said, "I guess the real strong one here is you."

So sometimes, the higher road opens before us, even when we are not actively seeking it.

We can seek the wisdom of the higher road in our religious and spiritual traditions.

Surely, the Sermon on the Mount counsels us to take the higher road:

When somebody forces you to go a mile, go the second mile. You've been taught to love your neighbor and hate your enemy, but I tell you to love your enemy. Pray for your enemy.

The Talmud is another manual on taking the higher road. Its teachings point us toward practical solutions for many of life's interpersonal problems, indicating the higher road with telling consistency. It is a handbook to life's troubling moral issues. When you have stolen from someone, what is fair compensation to make things right? If you have been stolen from, what should you demand in payback? The Talmud offers point-by-point instructions, and its wisdom is sound.

Such wisdom counsels us that we should never stoop to the same level as those who are hurting us but rather, raise our standard to a higher level. We always do better by seeking the higher path.

We can become as servants to our fellow people.

A few years ago we lamented the death, at age 87, of a woman named Elsie Schalit. I first met Elsie when I came to my church 31 years ago. At that point, she had already been a cherished vendor to Marble Collegiate Church for 45 years!

She and her husband owned a print shop, and they did our printing: the Sunday calendars, the stationery, and just about everything else. When her husband died in the 1970s, Elsie continued to work until her retirement in 1993. And they had started working for us in 1923! That means they served the church for 70 years all together, which says a lot about the quality of their work.

One special thing about Elsie was her complete orientation toward being a servant. She always wanted her work for us to be perfect. If the ink wasn't the right shade, she would happily take back the printing job and do another run. One winter weekend when we had a blizzard, Elsie came all the way in from Queens and trudged through the snow to make sure the printing plant delivered the Sunday bulletins.

When we adopt the servant mode, we are taking the higher road of life. It isn't easy.

We can refuse to expect thanks or rewards.

Taking the higher road offers its own reward. You may receive thanks or rewards for doing well by your fellow life travelers, or you may not. That is no matter! Step by step and decision by decision, you will see your life become empowered and transformed.

Deepening Our Understanding

Every day offers us countless opportunities to take the higher road. With awareness, commitment to the Golden Rule, and the right attitude, we can consistently take that higher path and see our lives transfigured:

- *Your perspective will be higher, wider, and more revealing.* New opportunities for action will unfold beneath you because your life will be built on a solid foundation of good acts and good deeds.

- *Bridges will be rebuilt, relationships healed.* Commitment to the higher path builds rewarding, unassailable human relationships.

The habit of taking the higher path, consistently in all things, brings new power and determination to any life.

18

Freedom Follows
Loving Ourselves

---

*I*n Chapter 13, we explored the topic of kindness, and as you have almost certainly noticed, that subject has emerged in other parts of this book too. There is a simple reason that it comes up so often: Practicing kindness frees us to operate on a higher plane in many areas of our lives. It lifts all our human relationships to that "higher road" where many more possibilities open before us.

In this chapter, we will explore another, no less important, aspect of kindness. It is the relevance of being kind to ourselves, of actually *loving* ourselves. When we are kind by understanding our own shortcomings and not being harsh in our self-judgments, we empower ourselves to act more freely in the world. Fairness to self frees us to transform our lives in new and dynamic ways.

When I was in junior high school, I was nominated to run for president of our homeroom class. A big deal in the seventh grade! But as the election approached, the buzz wasn't about who would be the best homeroom president.

The boy at the next desk leaned over to me and said, "Psst! Arthur, are you going to vote for yourself? Are you?"

Voting for yourself was assumed to be wrong. There was gossip that a sixth-grade girl had voted for herself the year before. People thought that was awful, and her reputation had suffered.

Even in seventh grade, my classmates had already absorbed the lesson that it is right to love others more than we love ourselves.

Religion can make this basic belief even stronger and more persuasive. When people mix the notion of a judgmental God into this equation, the result often goes something like this:

I must love God first, others second, and myself last.

But when we think about it, that doesn't make sense. Our ability to love God and other people can be measured by our effectiveness at loving ourselves. It *depends* on our ability to like ourselves. It has nothing to do with selfishness or egotism or lack of love for our fellow human beings. The better I am able to care for myself, the stronger I will be to care about and for others. This is called "benevolent self-interest."

Of course, love is a complicated subject. We want it more than anything else, and we all do our best to be loving. But most of us aren't very good at it when the object of our love and admiration is ourselves.

We need to stop and reconsider our self-imposed prohibition on loving ourselves. When we do, we realize that being incapacitated in the area of self-love brings some very crippling aftereffects:

- *Our self-esteem suffers.* Always putting other people first is a good prescription for a happy life. Yet feeling ourselves to be less worthy of love than other people is not healthy. Living with that assumption over time can train us to think of ourselves as second-class citizens in the human family. Fairness demands that, at the very least, we see ourselves as equals.

- *Our voices and ideas can become stifled, bottled up.* In years past, I have often come away from meetings and discussions with the realization that even though I had an idea or suggestion that was just as worthy as any that were discussed, I let mine get voted down, or slip away, without receiving the attention it deserved. In somewhat biblical prose, this might be termed "hiding your light under a bushel." If we sustain this pattern over long periods of time, we can become frustrated. We have tacitly agreed to always take second seat behind other people.

- *Our ability to lead suffers.* Of course, no one likes overbearing leaders who shout down the opposition and insist on having their way, no matter what. Yet the fact remains that true leaders, positive ones, such as Nelson Mandela, Ghandi, and Martin Luther King, Jr., respected themselves enough to communicate their vision to others.

- *We become free to take action in more ways in the world.* We become like the steersman who is empowered to direct his or her vessel where he or she wants to go in life. Self-respect and self-love function like the oil on the hinges of the great rudder of our lives. If it is missing, our ability to direct our lives becomes harder, or even impossible.

How can we overcome our well-learned belief that self-love and self-kindness are blameworthy activities? I have found that the following outlooks and practices help.

We can create personal time for reflection and self-healing.

We live in a world where it is often necessary to engage in an activity called "keeping up appearances." Even when we are in a state of inner turmoil, or dealing with some major challenge, we are expected to appear calm and untroubled. Sometimes, the weight of it all can become burdensome and terribly difficult to bear.

Of course, there are good reasons and justifications for "keeping up a good front" this way. We need to protect our need for privacy, especially when conducting our daily business and routine activities. When our parents are ill or we have just argued with our spouses or our children are experiencing difficulty, we cannot allow those problems to spill out at inappropriate times. No one likes it when we wear our feelings on our sleeves, always talking about our problems. But to pretend all is well when it is not and to conceal our pain and discomfort can be very hard on us. We are being unkind to ourselves in ways we would not be unkind to others.

The remedy is to take some quiet time to be kind to ourselves. I am not talking about passively lying around, with no positive thought activity taking place. Instead, I am talking about enjoying some quiet time to think about our current problems and challenges with an attitude of calm and self-forgiveness. It can be helpful to be in a quiet place (no one can arrive at a solution to a pressing problem while watching television, perhaps not even while listening to the radio) and make a conscious decision:

> *I am here for this quiet time to be kind and loving to myself and to try to work this challenge through.*

We know that the great spiritual leaders of the ages—from Buddha to Moses, from Mohammed to Jesus—all withdrew into the solitude of quiet spaces when facing stress and problems. I believe they were engaged in an active form of self-love. There is no reason we cannot follow their good example.

We can broaden our definition of love to include spiritual growth.

Let me turn again to a book called *The Road Less Traveled* by Scott Peck (Touchstone Books, 2003). He has written some of the best material on love and self-acceptance that I have ever come across.

In a chapter called "Love Is Not a Feeling," he says love can be defined in the following way:

To extend oneself for the purpose of nurturing one's own or another's spiritual growth.

Love is a means to spiritual growth. In this broader definition, we see why it encompasses many varieties of self-caring, including:

- Acceptance of our own shortcomings.

- A willingness to forgive ourselves for actions we have done, or left undone.

- A resilient determination to operate from a basis of what we believe and know to be good about ourselves. And not to tear ourselves down because of our shortcomings.

We can make healthy decisions about what we will and will not do.

Part of being loving to ourselves lies in consciously managing our own situation and deciding where we can make commitments and where a commitment would be inappropriate or overly taxing or would cut into our prior commitments to others.

In popular terms, this ability may become manifest in our ability to say no:

- When your boss insists that you complete a project by day's end and you know you cannot, self-love requires you to say so and negotiate for a solution that will not be so hard on you.

- When someone calls and asks you to make a commitment of your time to a charitable activity when you are already overextended, self-care means saying that you cannot do so.

In the end, making such healthy decisions, which are kind to yourself, are actually better for other people too. You are dealing with the world on a more realistic plane at the same time you are saving yourself from undue stress and strain.

Love to self is a way to nurture your soul.

We can put the "Three Ps" into practice.

When I find that I have been being unkind to myself, I often remind myself of a self-preserving routine that really works. I call it the "Three Ps," standing for *pace, peace,* and *perspective*:

- *Pace* means practicing thoughtful management of your day and your life. It is learning to move ahead with a deliberate speed, a speed that is right for you. A psychologist once told me, "Norman Vincent Peale is the best-paced man I have ever known." Dr. Peale, my friend and mentor at Marble Collegiate Church, lived a life of enormous demands. But I can attest to the fact that he set a deliberate inner pace that kept him from being crushed and frazzled by a very busy life.

- *Peace* means *inner* peace. It's developing a calm center. The Quakers speak of getting "centered," which I understand to mean getting in touch with the inner sanctuary of the soul, that quiet place within.

- *Perspective* is a process of stepping back and viewing things in their true relationship and importance. If we see things in their true position, we will often realize that what is really important is seldom an emergency, and emergencies are seldom important.

We can manage the "Three Ps" apart from the demands that others place on us.

There's a wonderful story about the great psychotherapist Carl Jung. When one of Jung's patients called to ask for an extra appointment, Jung told him he was too busy. Even when the man became angry and demanded that Jung see him at once, he replied that he was too busy to schedule an appointment. He had no time.

A few days later, the man was sailing along on Lake Zurich, where Jung lived. And he saw Jung sitting on the back wall of his property, completely relaxed, with his feet dangling in the water. When he returned home, that man called Jung to accuse him.

"You were not truthful with me!" he said.

"Indeed I was, " Jung replied. "I had an important appointment, with myself."

We can pay special attention to managing the emotions that are the hardest on us.

There are certain emotions that might be called literally "killers." They have just that much power to hurt us, even damage our health. Learning to manage them is an important component of practical self-love.

- *Anger.* This is a normal emotion and can be very helpful if understood and properly directed. If I lived in Germany in the years preceding World War II, for example, I would have been justifiably furious at my country, and at my leaders, and at my fellow citizens for what was taking place. If I were living in South Africa under apartheid, I would have been justifiably wrathful at my nation's official policies of containment and prejudice. So there are healthy forms of anger, varieties that urge us to act.

  Other varieties of anger are less positive, causing us to do harm to ourselves and to others as well. Road rage is not self-loving. Anger at former spouses, former friends, and other "formers" who have hurt us is something that we need to process and release. Anger at ourselves, above all other forms of anger, needs to be dissipated. When we hate ourselves for things we have done in the past, we are literally introducing a powerful poison into our own system. No good can come of it.

- *Jealousy.* Here is another extraordinarily powerful emotion. Evolutionary psychologists tell us that jealousy evolved because of our need to protect our mates and partners. They even tell us that some degree of jealousy about our loved ones might be a healthy attitude that acknowledges the fact that our partners are desirable and worthy of our love.

  More often, jealousy is a foundationless wrath that harms us and others around us. Jealousy is the leading cause of murder in the world. It is the leading contributor to domestic violence. When it gains a hold over us, it can be very hard to shake loose from its power. When we feel jealousy's power, we owe it to ourselves and those around us to consider its roots and process it appropriately.

- *Resentment.* Do you know anybody who isn't living with some kind of resentment? It is like a poison. When it gets into the system and does its work, it can contribute to any number of emotional and physical illnesses. If we could eliminate resentment, hospitals might close whole wings, and pharmaceutical companies would wonder what happened to their once-booming businesses.

- *Desire for vengeance.* This is resentment's closest ally. When we feel we have been wronged or harmed, how eager we can be to get even. When we fall victim to the lure of this powerful emotion, we often are injured more than the person we want to harm. The Bible is so right: "'Vengeance is mine,' says the Lord." We don't have to worry about getting back at somebody. Life has a way of doing that on its own." The Vedic laws of Karma teach us a similar lesson. Since in the end, the universe seeks its own equilibrium, we can remind ourselves to gently let go of the desire for retribution and turn our minds again to greater truths.

We can be true to our gifts.

I suggest you ask yourself whether you are more like a moth or an eagle. They are both creatures that fly and decide where they want to go. But beyond that, there are few similarities.

Let us say that on a summer evening, you're reading indoors by a lamp and a moth flies into the room. Where does it go? It aims for the hot light and moves dangerously toward self-destruction.

So often in relationships or in life situations, we are like moths. We keep going back, going back into unkind situations, over and over. We are acting self-destructively, and we become consumed by the very thing we thought we were going to solve or master.

Another thing to remember is that a moth never learns. It goes on trying to destroy itself until it finally succeeds or cripples itself to the point at which flight becomes impossible.

In contrast to the moth, are you an eagle learning to fly free? I have a favorite eagle story.

One day, a naturalist was walking in the country when he passed a farm. In the chicken yard was a half-grown eagle pecking at the feed along with the chickens. So the naturalist went to the farmer and asked, "Why is there an eagle living with the chickens?"

"Oh, well," the farmer answered, "when the eagle was very young, he fell in with the chickens, and now he's got chicken ways."

The naturalist asked the farmer if he could try to work with the eagle and bring him to his true self. The farmer agreed. So the naturalist picked the eagle up, held him as high as he could, and cried out, "You're an eagle. You're an eagle. You're the king of the birds. You deserve to fly free. Fly!" The eagle looked about, then jumped back down with the chickens.

The next day, the naturalist took the eagle to the roof of the farmhouse. He whispered in his ear, "You're an eagle. You're king of the birds. You were intended to fly free. Fly!" The eagle looked around a bit. He saw some open sky, but right below him he saw his old familiar situation. And he returned to it.

On the third day, the naturalist took the eagle to a mountaintop, and with strength and conviction he held the bird high. "You are an eagle. You were created to fly free: God made you to cover the skies." The eagle looked up and saw the limitless sky all around. Then he woke up to who he was and flew away.

Are you flying into the fire like a moth? Are you an eagle confining yourself to the chicken yard? Or are you learning to fly free?

God can help you in this regard. Note the words of Isaiah when he said:

> *Those who wait on the Lord will renew their strength.*
> *They will mount up on wings as the eagle. They will run*
> *and not be weary. They will walk and faint not.*

Are you being kind to yourself? Are you loving and nurturing yourself as well as you do others? Learn to love yourself, and as you do, your ability to love both God and other people will be enhanced. And, my friends, you will fly free.

Deepening Our Understanding

Loving kindness can become a high road we take in our lives. With the right attitude and outlook, we discover that love is made up of two distinct parts: love for others, and love for ourselves.

Kindness and forgiveness are the action-oriented parts of love. When we learn that it is appropriate to direct them at ourselves, we discover unique and remarkable gifts in our lives:

- We accord ourselves the same justifiable respect that we direct toward other people.

- Our self-esteem soars as our ideas, plans, and visions become reality.

- Our ability to lead soars as we become better able to take free, energetic action in the world.

As I read over those last three points that describe the benefits of self-love and self-acceptance, a question comes immediately to my mind. Why wouldn't I decide to live my life in such a remarkable, productive way? Given the option, why wouldn't I make such a positive choice? Of course I would, and that decision all begins with the simple first step of deciding to love myself as I love others.

19

Freedom Follows Cultivating a Loving Heart

---

*I*f there is a term I use in this book that requires clarification, a *loving heart* might well be it.

Is a loving heart a heart that is consumed with the desire to direct acceptance and affection at all people? Is it one that shuts no one out? One that directs its owner to do good in the world?

Yes, it is all those things, and more. It is a heart that is so vast and tender and kind that it easily encompasses the entire world, and all its people, with warmth and caring and love.

While I was getting my hair cut one morning, my barber Paul and I were chatting about what a lovely morning it was. Paul, a soft-spoken and gentle man, told me that he had stopped on his way to work to spend a few quiet minutes sitting on a bench in a nearby park, just to enjoy the day.

"It was so pleasant," he said, "except for the pigeons."

Then he quickly caught himself and added, "Well, I guess they have a right to live too."

That was a nice touch. That conversation reminded me of something I experienced some years ago, directly across the street from the United Nations building in New York. I was walking along when I noticed a small group of people standing on the sidewalk. I stopped too and found that they were watching a sick pigeon that was huddled against a building. That pigeon looked like all birds do when they are very ill. Its head seemed to be telescoped down into its body. Its feathers were fluffed. It was shivering.

The whole scene resembled a pathetic deathwatch but for one thing: Standing next to the sick bird was another pigeon. That second bird seemed to be watching over its sick friend, keeping vigil. To me, the presence of that second bird seemed a moving symbol, especially across the street from the United Nations. It seemed to embody the image of a strong nation caring for a weak nation. Or possibly it was a simple message that a strong individual should offer solace to another person who is troubled.

That image makes me think of the centrality of love. Love is principal, love is pivotal. Love is the central reality in the way the universe works.

I feel inspired and uplifted every time I recall words that Teilhard de Chardin wrote about love in his book *The Phenomenon of Man* (Perennial Books, 1966):

> *The day will come, after we have harnessed the energies of space, wind, tides and gravity, that we will harvest the energies of love. And for the second time in the history of the world, we will have discovered fire.*

I've also been inspired time and time again by the words of Saint Paul, recorded in that magnificent, eloquent, brilliant, and powerful essay on love we know as Corinthians 13:1. I'm paraphrasing, but these are the statements Paul makes about love:

> *I may have all the money, all the power, all the prestige. I may be an earth-mover. I may have so much faith I can make incredible things happen. I may be talented. I may be beautiful. I may be charming. I may be witty. I may be persuasive. I may have all these things. But if I don't have love, all of those remarkable things are nothing more than banging on a noisy cymbal.*

Without love we have nothing. Our lives become impaired in countless ways:

- *We see only the worst in people.* Love opens our eyes to all that is good; we see and accept people "warts and all," as the popular saying goes. Without love, we dwell on other people's shortcomings and faults. Love, sure and certain, leads our steps onto those "higher roads" we have visited often in this book.

- *We alienate others.* When love is resident in our hearts, people sense it and are drawn to us. They also sense the opposite. When we lack love, we become judgmental, prejudiced, opinionated, dismissive, and mean-spirited.

- *Without meaning to, we harm the world.* Lack of love translates into countless small acts of unkindness, every day. We are unkind to the people we pass in the street, unkind to our children, unkind to ourselves. The effect is cumulative. Over time, we contribute more than we realize to building a cold and uncaring world.

- *We lose our ability to accomplish great things in the world.* All positive changes the world has seen have taken place through the force of love. I know that is quite a statement, but I earnestly believe it to be true. Wars and hatred did not build the great cathedrals and mosques and synagogues of the world, nor did they create great poetry or music or art. Love did those things. The power of love is unimaginably greater than the power of rancor.

But what if love is lacking in your life? What if you'd like to enjoy all the benefits of love but don't know where to start?

You can begin to invite more of that love into your life by cultivating a *loving heart.* I can recommend a few steps to help that happen. The first step is quite simple.

We can cultivate the art of paying attention.

Learn to pay attention to other people. Pay attention to their needs. Pay attention to where they are on their life's journey.

How often we fail to do that! Just this week, a friend told me a story that illustrates the importance of paying attention.

It seems that when Calvin Coolidge was running for president, he was invited to an elegant dinner party. He could stay for only part of the evening before he had to leave for another commitment. After Coolidge had left, people started to discuss whether or not he was going to be elected president. The general consensus was that he wouldn't make it.

The lone dissenter was a little girl, about 8 years old. She was convinced that Coolidge was not only going to be elected hands-down but that he would also be a very good president. When someone asked her why, she said, "Because he's the only one who noticed the Band-Aid on my finger."

So there's the art of paying attention, the art of noticing. What does this story suggest to us? Many things about the art of paying attention.

Lovers should notice their lovers. Friends should notice their friends. Husbands should notice their wives. Wives, notice their husbands. Parents, notice what is going on in the lives of their children. Children, as they grow up, should notice what's happening in the lives of their parents. Employers should notice what is happening in their employees' lives. Employees should notice what is going on in the lives of their bosses. Strangers should even notice strangers—the people they sit next to on the train, the people who wait on them in stores.

Keep noticing and paying attention. Remain aware of what is going on.

We can refresh and renew our powers of observation.

Every time I tell the following story, it gets a strong reaction. It seems that there once was an Iowa farmer whose wife kept complaining because her husband never told her that he loved her. So one day at Sunday lunch, the husband sat up erect at the table. And he said, "I have an announcement to make. Twenty years ago I told you that I loved you. If anything changes, I will let you know."

Now that's a funny story. Everyone laughs at it. But the fact that we all laugh means that it reveals something of a problem, doesn't it? It contains the lesson that we need to pay attention to the people around us. We must learn to notice.

We can question our own point of view in the light of others'.

Last year, I had a bona fide confrontation with my wonderful assistant, Susan Eldred. I felt that she was taking too long with some editing work that was on her desk. In response, I made very big mistake. I suggested how she could better use her time. I attempted to reorganize things for her. It was an immense, insensitive mistake.

Susan is a woman who always exudes joy, but when she came to work the next day, she was sober and sullen and joyless. About halfway through the day, I said, "Susan, we need to talk."

And she said, "We sure do."

She then began to explain how difficult it can be to run my office. She said, "Let's just take the telephone. That phone is always ringing. And when that phone rings, I know that I represent you. You want me to treat people graciously, with understanding and compassion. I do that, and I take time with people. I'm not curt, I'm not short. I'm very caring. And when people call who'd like to explore getting married here, I spend a lot of time with them. Shouldn't I? I want them to know that this is a very friendly, loving church to be in. But, Arthur, these things take time. And I also handle correspondence—and so many other things. And I'm always responsive when you come to me and say, 'I have a problem. Can you stop what you are doing and help me out with it?'"

Do you know something? She was absolutely right. Susan's words made me realize I wasn't paying attention to her. I was only interested in my own point of view. I really didn't notice what she was doing. I was wrong to do that.

Yet how often do we minimize those people around us, people who are doing enormous things to help us? We take them for granted. My conversation with Susan made me realize that I had to do something to reduce her workload. And I've got some work to do.

That's the art of paying attention and being willing to reconsider where we stand. Noticing is an expression of love.

We can simply be there for other people.

One other powerful way to bring more love into your life is to cultivate the practice of *being there* for other people, much like that healthy pigeon was there to watch over its sick friend.

I know some of you may be saying, "That's a good idea, but what about me? What about *my* needs? Why should I be there for other people when they are seldom there for me?"

I have a simple answer to those questions. If you are there for other people, the world is going to work out things so that other people will always be there for you.

We can practice acts of caring and love.

It is possible to do so, even in the most unforgiving circumstances.

During the early days of the Iraq war, I read many stories in the news that reflected the fact that American soldiers stationed there were not certain of the role they were expected to take when interacting with Iraqi civilians. Mistakes were made, some of them very costly to members of the American military and Iraqi civilians alike.

One story I heard on a television news program really stood out for me as an example of how it is possible to be caring and to express human concern, even across such vast linguistic and cultural borders.

It seems that one Friday, hundreds of Iraqi civilians were going to a mosque to pray. American soldiers, unfamiliar with Islamic holy practices, stopped them on the road, which triggered a hostile reaction. People on both sides were scared.

First, in an effort to intimidate the Iraqis, the soldiers pointed their guns into the air as a warning. That did not calm things down! Both sides became tense. But then the American officer in charge made a remarkable decision after he realized that these were simple people on their way to worship, not people who meant them harm.

He ordered his soldiers to kneel down and take the posture of people who were praying, which they did. The tension was released as soon as the civilians saw this action, which spoke to them in a language stronger than words. It was an expression of human sympathy and caring.

That is a very moving story for me. It shows that caring and love are instantly recognizable as a means of communication between people, even in harsh and unforgiving circumstances.

We can allow other people to express love for us through blessings.

In recent years, I have been experiencing macular degeneration—a troubling, gradual deterioration of my eyesight.

One day not long ago in a meeting at Marble Collegiate Church, a woman on our staff asked me if I would like to receive a laying-on of hands from everyone there. It was a way for everyone to bless me and express their support and concern for me in regard to my problem.

I agreed. I went and stood in the middle of the group. People said prayers, and then they placed their hands on me in a gesture of support and healing. It was very moving for me, an expression of thoughtful and profound care.

I have been in similar blessings when other people have received the thoughts, the prayers, the blessings too. And I know that at such times, everyone present feels the blessing, the healing, and a remarkable uplifting power.

We can bless others, sight unseen.

I'd like to tell you about something that has made an enormous difference in my life. It goes like this:

> *Wherever you go, bless someone. Whatever you're doing, bless someone. Whomever you're with, bless that person.*

As you're walking down the street, look at each person you see and silently say, "Bless you. Bless you, bless you, bless you, bless you."

At work, look at the person at the next desk, even the mean-est-spirited person, and think, "Bless you. Bless you."

Even if you have the stingiest, nastiest boss, think, "Bless you. Bless you. Bless you. Bless you."

If you try this, you will find that two things will happen for you. First, you will uplift others. You never know when some mysterious power will take your blessing, which really is a prayer, and begin to work behind the scenes to make that other person's life better. Second, when you enter into the spirit of blessing everyone you come across, you are also going to be blessed. You will be uplifted and happy. You will make someone's day as you make your own.

Deepening Our Understanding

Let me share with you one last observation about love. An incredible fact: Love is the one thing that increases to the degree that we give it away. The more love we give to other people, the more there will be for us, and the fuller our lives will be:

- *We accomplish great things more easily.* A person acting alone can never be as strong, or as effective, as many people acting in concert. With a loving heart, we draw people to ourselves and grow stronger and freer in all we do.

- *Our love will open us up to all that is good in other people.* When love replaces harsh judgment, new doors open before us. We come to see abilities and strengths we had never noticed before.

Love enables us to help the world and all around us in countless ways, both big and small. Love enables us to accomplish all we can and empowers those around us to become all they desire to be.

20

Freedom Means Embracing the Future

*W*e have two choices regarding the future. We can resist the future, fear it, and recoil from it. Or we can embrace tomorrow and welcome what it will bring.

Reaching out toward tomorrow with eagerness and enthusiasm is not always easy. The future will surely bring things we will not like. Yet whatever we feel about the future, it will arrive! We cannot change that, but we can do something even better. We can change our attitude about it. We can greet the future with open arms and enthusiasm.

The decisions we make in this area of life can make all the difference.

The day after I graduated from high school, my family moved from where I had been born and raised to a city and state nearly 800 miles away. The idea of moving excited me. I had never been more than 300 miles from home. I had the urge to travel, to see the country and the world. This was a first step. A new life was opening up before me.

But once we arrived at our new home, I was surprised at my reaction. This new future was not what I expected.

For the first few nights I cried myself to sleep. A profound sadness had overtaken me. I missed everybody and everything. I couldn't wait to get back and see everybody again, to pick up my life where it had left off.

The next summer, my father let me borrow his car for a trip back home. Nobody could have been more excited than I was.

But I was in for a big shock. When I got home, everything looked the same. My friends greeted me warmly and genuinely.

But something was different. Something was missing. I became aware that what was missing was me. I was no longer a part of the fabric of their lives. I had moved on, as they in their own ways had moved on.

I learned two things from this experience. First, that people are always in the process of changing. We can never count on people or places being the same as we remember them.

And second, I realized that if I wanted to have a fulfilled and happy life, I would have to adapt to those changes. I learned that the one constant of life is change. Change is permanent. When we fail to accept this reality, we do great damage to ourselves:

- *We stiffen and become rigid.* When we become mired in the ways and attitudes of the past, new events have a way of rolling right over us.

- *We fail to prepare and manage our lives well.* Instead of saying, "This is the next stage of my life, and this is what I need to do to get ready for it," we avoid the topic. This is a very harmful, very dangerous way of living our lives.

- *We arrive at a distorted view of ourselves.* People who resist the future end up creating false images and roles for themselves.

How much better, and more vibrant, it is to embrace the future. There is little more beautiful to see than a person who reaches his or her late years with a keen thirst for all that is new and happening in the world.

How can we develop that outlook? How can we welcome the future into our lives with open arms and eager hearts?

We can cultivate a desire to know what tomorrow brings.

Probably my first lesson in the inevitability and even the advantages of change happened when I was a little boy. My father had just bought a brand-new car. It was a Ford, and a car beyond all cars. It was the first year cars were designed without a running board. The headlights and the fenders were fused beautifully into the body of the car so that everything was sleek, modern, and aerodynamic. It was beautiful. I had never seen anything like it. To me it was the design to end all designs.

The next year Ford came out with a new model, quite different from the "ultimate model" of the previous year. I remember asking my father, "Daddy, do you like your car?"

"Yes," he responded.

"Is it a good car?"

He said, "It's as good as a car can be."

"Then why," I asked, "did they change it?"

I don't remember his answer. But I remember the lesson I learned. In order for things to improve, they must change. Since then I have been confronted with this fact over and over. I see how important it is to expect change and adjust to it. I see how, when we resist change, we put ourselves and others at a disadvantage.

I sometimes think about the song from the musical *Oklahoma!*, "Everything's Up to Date in Kansas City." It is a funny song about how modern everything is in that city, how all the progress and innovation that could ever happen have already occurred, from tall buildings to all the modern conveniences.

We often think in a similar way when we are trying to adjust to change. We deny that change is necessary or even possible.

You have probably heard some or all of the following statements, which have become popular with preachers and other people who speak in public:

- In the 1890s, a famous British scientist said that it was impossible to create a flying machine. Anything heavier than air could never get off the ground.

- At about the same time, a highly placed official in the U.S. Patent Office said that his agency was about to close its doors. Every possible invention had already been created.

- Harry Warner, the head of Warner Brothers, said that there would never be a market for talking movies. Why would anyone ever want to hear actors talk?

Whatever the mind can conceive can be achieved. We are wise to avoid saying something is impossible. The "impossible" has happened too often down through the ages. We may say something is unlikely or improbable, but we must never say *never*.

We can challenge our assumptions and beliefs.

Unless we know we are standing on a rock-solid truth, when there is a challenge to our ideas and point of view, we had better give consideration to changing our minds. Otherwise, life will sweep over us and take us down.

A number of years ago Mount Saint Helens, the volcano in the state of Washington, was giving every sign of erupting. One night, an elderly man who had lived on that mountain for all of his life was being interviewed on television.

He wasn't afraid of any catastrophe! No lava was going to come down on him! He knew that mountain. He knew its moods and everything else about it.

He was advised to get off the mountain, but he refused. He couldn't imagine seeing anything he had not seen in the past. Yet a few days later, lava poured down and took his life. If he had changed his mind, he would have saved his life and have also encouraged his own internal growth by questioning his own certainty.

We can understand what the future will bring, not avoid it.

I find it interesting, and revealing, that some people have a negative reaction around the issues of writing their wills and planning their estates. They seem to believe that if they never talk about death or dying, they will get "off the hook" and be exempt.

This kind of thinking permeates so much of our resistance to change:

- "I don't have the courage to talk to my daughter about what safe, responsible sex means," a parent told me not long ago. Does this person expect that daughter to remain celibate forever? This parent may procrastinate forever, but that will not prevent that daughter's eventual love life. Only action, not avoidance, will allow that parent to exert a positive influence on what will take place.

- "I'm allowing my mother to live alone in her home, even though she is in severely declining health," a man told me. He is not taking any rational precautions about what might happen to her: not having help in the home, not installing new railings on stairs. Nothing. It is as though he believes that he can prevent the future from coming by failing to prepare.

- "I knew I needed to have the timing belt replaced in my car when it hit 100,000 miles," a friend told me recently. "But I put it off, and at 110,000 miles, it broke and destroyed my engine. I guess I was hoping to get lucky."

What will happen, will happen. Rational preparation is a practical way to reduce the negative consequences that the future will exert on our lives.

We can commit ourselves to growth.

There is a famous story about Fred Astaire. It seems that he received some very negative comments after one of his earliest auditions. The people who auditioned him said simply that he couldn't dance, and he could only sing a little.

Years later, Astaire had those words, "Can't dance. Can sing a little." posted over his mantle, where he could look at them. It is clear that Astaire didn't allow himself to become discouraged by others' opinions of him. Instead, he *grew*. And he was able to change.

Rollo May, the great thinker and writer, often addresses the subject of change in his books. He dwells on the incredible, revolutionary changes in the last part of the twentieth century. May has said that there is no precedent in history for what is happening in the world today. Therefore, there are no guidelines for us to move through these changes. But he also notes that some people find change exhilarating, not frightening.

After all, we live in a time of great opportunity. Old forms, dated and irrelevant, are being replaced by new and refreshing ones. It can be a much better world.

Oh, for the possibilities of being a part of creating something new! The first step is to commit ourselves to growth, see ourselves as souls that are emerging, evolving, developing, unfolding.

We can stretch ourselves to the point where we see ourselves as people who are open to process and who have the courage to experience something new.

We can accept the reality that change will not be easy.

In a world that is moving and changing so quickly, we need to remind ourselves to grow and stretch. There will be discomfort. But if we avoid the pain of change, there won't be any gain. We will only become rigid and unchanging as the world rushes by.

We can have faith.

Remember that the rock of life, the foundation that is unchangeable, is the higher power. It is what so many of us call God. Trust in that power and you will gain the strength to trust change to bring a bounty of good things to your life.

Deepening Our Understanding

When we resist the reality that tomorrow will come, we become rigid, tight, unproductive, and unprepared. Yet with initiative and gumption, we can become bigger and more robust in our view and learn to welcome the future and what it will bring.

The benefits are great indeed:

- *We become flexible.* We claim our innate ability to adapt happily to whatever life places before us.

- *We become masters of life's great transitions.* Middle age, old age, changes of career—none of these hold any terror if we adapt to the flow and rhythm of life and the changes it brings.

- *We grow and come to know ourselves better.* None of us is the same person we were when we were children. The process of living has deepened and changed and enriched each one of us. By embracing the changes around us, we will better understand the changes within us.

A thirst for the future and its changes is the greatest freeing force for the human heart. It is the power that lets us move ahead to each new day with decisiveness and courage.

21

Freedom Follows
Giving Thanks

---

*O*n Thanksgiving and many other days of the year, we like to give thanks for all the good things we have in our lives. And when something truly wonderful happens—our children win awards, we get a promotion—life seems so uplifting that we stop and say, "I owe thanks for this."

There is another way to give thanks too. We practice it less frequently than giving thanks for good things, yet it offers greater opportunities for growth. I am talking about giving thanks for the challenges that life places in our paths. It is very difficult to do. How it tests us! But in the end, this outlook brings freedom and personal growth.

Some years ago, two of my closest friends were driving home behind a truck near the Delaware Water Gap on the border of New Jersey and Pennsylvania. Without warning, the truck veered to the left, grazed the divider, careened across the highway, and flipped over. My friends hit the brakes, stopped on the shoulder of the highway, and got out of their car. They were shocked at what they saw. The cab of the truck was crushed. All its windows were broken. They thought the worst, that the driver must have been killed. But then something extraordinary occurred. The driver came crawling out of the wreckage. His clothes were torn, and he was bleeding from a cut on his face, but he was alive. He staggered up to a standing position, looked at the truck, and began to repeat, "Thank God, Thank God, Thank God . . ."

Now, that man was someone uniquely equipped to offer thanks in the face of life's calamities and near disasters. Instead of dwelling on the horror of it all, his first reaction was to give thanks that he was still alive.

We can do something similar too in our daily lives. When faced with challenges, we can say, "I thank this adversity because it brings me an opportunity to grow." Often, the major impediments to practicing this outlook are our own egos and our placing blame on other people.

- *Our egos.* We like to cast ourselves in the role of "starring hero" who can conquer any problem, who knows just what to do. Even when we are shaken, we don't like to admit it. That is a pattern that stifles our ability to grow through our troubles.

- *Our love of placing the blame elsewhere.* It is so seductive to characterize all of life's challenges as unfair: the "this is not fair!" game. When we get into the habit of believing we are the targets of all life's ills, we are only avoiding the responsibility of doing the difficult work that is required to process our setbacks and learn from them.

Instead, we need to learn to welcome life's challenges, to see them as growth opportunities. Unless we practice this outlook, some very damaging themes emerge in our lives:

- *We finally accept the role of victim.* Everyone has problems. Everyone is the victim of experiences they wish had never come their way. Yet some of us weave those events into negative scripts for our lives ("First my father died, then I wasted 8 years in a dead-end job, then my marriage went on the rocks . . . ") while others of us don't allow life's tests to color our outlook in that way. The latter group of people have the knack of not only surviving challenges but seeking the knowledge they bring.

- *We overlook opportunities to learn and grow.* When we stiffen and try not to think about our problems, we cease to learn. In effect, we move at least half of life's experiences to the margins of our lives, out of consideration. That's not a productive way to go through life. Our success hinges on our ability to learn from everything.

- *Finally, our world outlook becomes out of kilter, skewed.* Curiously, people who try to hide from the work of processing life's challenges don't grow more attuned to the good things in life. They don't become more positive, even though you might expect them to. Instead, they take more and more of the good things life brings them and mischaracterize them as bad. They make statements like "I'm getting married again? Hope it works this time!" and "My son got into medical school? So what. Big deal! I don't think he's ready to work that hard." Since negativism always breeds more negativism, the wrong attitude can overrun our lives and rob the joy from everything around it.

What can we do when we face challenges we would rather avoid? How can we learn to welcome the growth they promise and even give thanks for them?

We can get our egos out of the way.

Many years ago, I was having a conflict with another man. It all started when he said something very caustic and critical about me. He wasn't talking behind my back; he had the disarming gumption to deliver his criticism point blank, right into my face. In fact, his criticism was directed at an area of my life where I felt especially weak. And how that hurt.

For a very long time, that experience virtually crippled me. Even when I hadn't seen this man for weeks, I was still stewing about him. In fact, I was spending my time making mental lists of all his weaknesses and shortcomings. Who was he to talk to me that way? He wasn't perfect!

I was so angry. Then one day I decided to talk the problem over with a trusted friend. The first words he said only made me feel worse: "Arthur, is there any truth to what that man said?"

I didn't want to think about that! But I reluctantly admitted that, yes, there was some truth in what my attacker had said.

"Then why don't you get your ego out of the way, swallow your pride, and thank him for what he told you?" my friend said. "Tell him you will use his criticism as an incentive to try to grow in the area he mentioned."

That was very difficult advice to accept, and even harder to follow, but I did it. I went to my "adversary," and I told him I had been thinking about what he had said to me and that I was grateful for it. Now, that man might not have been taking a "higher road" when he criticized me. He might have been mean-spirited and hateful. That is probably not for me to judge, but I do know for certain that my experience with him taught me an important lesson about humility. When you have the courage to get your ego out of your way, you open up to countless new learning opportunities.

We can be thankful and turn disappointment to growth.

Many years ago when my son Paul was 12, he taught me a remarkable lesson about learning from life's setbacks. He had been working so hard in science that year. He knew in his heart that he would capture that year's prize as the best science student in his grade. He had earned A's. He had done extra work. Then, when the final assembly of the year came and he was sitting there expecting the principal to call him up to accept the award, someone else's name was called instead of his.

Paul came to me with tears in his eyes. But then Paul said something that astonished me: "Do you think they'd let me sit in on classes over the summer? If I learned enough, maybe I can win the award next year."

Faced with disappointments, some of us seem to disintegrate. Others of us, like Paul, have a desire to keep growing despite setbacks. We are oriented toward growth.

Such setbacks almost always offer us chances to advance. In ways large or small, there is always a choice to either back away and shut down or regroup and move forward. For example, when you fail a driver's test, a certification test, or any other exam, you can call the test unfair and flawed, or you can think of yourself as stupid and incompetent. Or you can praise the test for drawing your attention to an area where you needed to work and grow stronger. When your spouse criticizes you for being inattentive, you can become angry and defensive, or you can offer thanks for the criticism and work to grow in the level of care you bring to your loving relationship.

The choice is yours. It can make all the difference between growing and staying small as you go through life.

We can be thankful for the opportunity to try new things.

Not long ago, a physician friend of mine told me an interesting story. His son, who had been in the premed program at Harvard and hoping to follow in his father's footsteps, had recently decided to make a change of career plans. He would drop out of the premed program.

He had given it his best try. He had tried hard and then still harder, but medicine did not seem to be a "fit" for him. But he was a smart young man because he was flexible. He could have kept trying to force his way through the problem, but instead, he found a way around it. He now plans to be a research scientist, and I'll wager that he will be an excellent one who will make his mark on many people's lives in a profession that suits him so well.

When faced with adversity and problems, we are told we should keep trying again and again. That's good advice, except that when we try the wrong thing over and over again, the frustration that results can sap our desire to go on. As a wise person once observed:

If you keep trying the same thing, you tend to get the same results.

For this reason, we need to cultivate the habit of being playful and flexible when dealing with the obstacles that life places in our paths. One of my favorite illustrations of this principle is a story of something that happened to me some years ago. It is the story of a little ant.

Many years ago, I went camping with my family in the Grand Teton National Park in Wyoming, one of the most beautiful places I have ever visited. I went out early one morning to look at the snow-covered mountains across the lake from where we were staying. It was truly awe inspiring. But then I happened to look down, and near my feet where I was standing I saw an ant. He was moving ahead with such speed and momentum that I decided to test him a little. I placed a little hill of sand in his path to see how he would get around it. He walked up and over it. No problem for him! Next, I dug a little hole in front of him. In and out he went again, no problem. But then I put a stone in his path. He tried to climb it, tumbled off, then went around it. Finally, I placed a stick in front of him. A real challenge! He nearly butted into it, but then he changed direction, and with a few more attempts, he finally found his way around one end. And on he went.

He kept trying, but he did so flexibly. I think his lesson is an important one for us as we seek to move our lives ahead around obstacles. We can decide, rather than continuing to butt our heads against our problems, to try different approaches and angles until we find the path that is best for us. We can be thankful for the opportunity to try new things and learn.

We can be thankful for advice, but also thankful for our own solutions.

We enjoy access to so many sources of help today! Psychologists and therapists stand ready to help us understand our problems and find answers that are right for us. Friends make suggestions, as do parents, aunts and uncles, and authors of popular self-help books. Help has never been more available.

Seeking assistance in overcoming our difficulties is important and can provide new, useful insights. Yet it is important to make dealing with problems a personal process, even if that requires time and laborious thought.

A story from the Sufi Muslim tradition tells us about the dangers of opting for easy solutions. The story is about a cobbler who was once in such intense pain that he went to visit a physician, who proclaimed, "There is nothing that can help you." But in a few days, the cobbler reappeared at the doctor's door to report the good news that he was completely cured and free of all pain.

"How did you achieve this?" the doctor asked.

"It was simple!" the man replied. "I ate beans and drank vinegar, and as you can see, I am fine now!"

A few days later, the doctor was visited by a tailor who was extremely ill. This time, the physician had a solution. "Eat beans and drink vinegar!" he said. The tailor did as he was told, but he only grew sicker and sicker until he, too, found his own cure.

The moral of this little tale is clear:

Solutions that work for other people's problems will not necessarily work for yours.

Each of us has to find our own way. And sometimes the solutions that are best for us are not very pleasant. Nevertheless, there is no avoiding the work of addressing our problems, facing up to them, and arriving at our own solutions.

We can allow ourselves time.

We live in an age when "quick fixes" to problems are thought to be better than slow ones. Of course, that is sometimes true. If you go to the hospital with an appendicitis attack, you want a quick diagnosis so that you can become free of the pain at once.

But most of life's problems are different. Most are complex and require time:

- Time to understand the problem

- Time to let its deeper meanings unfold

- Time to learn to accept the problem

- Time to get good counsel and advice

- Time to plan what you will do

- Time to absorb the deeper lessons of the problem

- Time, finally, to learn to understand the full scope of the challenge you are facing

- Time to understand how meeting the challenge can lead you to a higher, more evolved life

Deepening Our Understanding

When problems confront us, our first response is often to dig in, deny, and exclaim, "Why me? This is unfair."

Another, more growthful, path lies open before us: that of honoring life's challenges and heeding the deeper meanings they bring.

When we turn our steps toward this higher path, our lives are transformed in remarkable ways:

- *We take responsibility for our lives.* We are in control, seeing ourselves as victims no more.

- *We orient ourselves toward improvement and growth.*
  No one can reach his or her fullest potential by hiding
  from life's greatest challenges. By overcoming them,
  we become extraordinary.

- *We become positive realists.* Does life hold challenges?
  Of course it does! But does that mean our lives are
  outside of our control, that we can only be tossed about
  by adversity? Not at all! When we run to and not from
  our difficulties, we become "overcomers." We become
  extraordinarily free to direct our lives with confidence
  and calm.

22

Freedom Follows
a Positive Attitude

*T*here are so many areas in our lives where we cannot be completely free. Much as we might like, we cannot completely control everything we do at work. At home, dozens of duties pull us away from what we would most like to be doing on any given day. In the larger scheme of our lives, money, or the lack of it, limits our latitude to do what we want, when we want to. And in our approach to our major life goals—the big visions, like novels we'd like to write, foundations we'd like to start, causes we'd like to help—we often have to zigzag around many roadblocks.

It is frustrating to discover that we are not free in so many areas of our lives. Yet there is one area in which we are completely, wonderfully free—that area is *attitude* in our lives.

Attitude is different from everything else in our lives. No one can ever tell us what kind of attitude to have. It is the one area of life where we are in complete, total control.

And attitude is also the groundwork we place beneath everything else we do in life. A bad attitude is like a crumbling, poorly made foundation under a house. No matter what we construct above it, everything stays weak. In contrast, a good attitude is like a massive stone foundation. A house built on such a base laughs at the winds and tremors that shake other buildings. This house can be noble, beautiful, and inspiring. It can be anything its owner hopes it to be because it rests on something so strong. And it is a unique reflection of the person who has built it.

I like to tell a story about a very beloved, erudite rabbi who had spent his life praying and studying the Scriptures. One day, one of his followers came to see him and said, "I need help! I don't know how to live out my faith in the marketplace where I work."

"Can you tell me about what life is like there?" the rabbi asked.

"There is only backbiting and bickering," the man replied. Then he went on to describe a whole series of negatives about his daily life.

And do you know what that rabbi did? Because he had no solution to offer that man, all he could do was cry.

But in his own way, the rabbi had answered the question. By crying, he gave an answer of compassion. I can empathize with him because I too feel the frustrations that rabbi felt when people say to me, "Arthur, my daily life is soulless and horrible. I am so frustrated. It is out of my control. What can I do?" Like that rabbi, I often can offer little more than sympathy and support.

But then I do something that really helps. I try to impart the one tool that any person really needs to live life more effectively on a day-to-day basis. I am talking about attitude.

Attitude is a tremendous resource that we seem to make so little use of. We have a gift. We have a fire. We have a light. We have something to give. We have been given an ability we can use to change our internal environment and the environment all around us too. That "something" is a positive attitude, and nothing compares to the effectiveness it brings to our lives.

You have surely noticed that when we take the opposite path and become mired in negative thinking, we do inestimable damage to ourselves:

- *We miss countless opportunities every day because we are so blinded by our bad outlook.* I recently read an anecdote about a woman who went into a routine meeting at work one morning and was terribly upset to see that her company president, a hard-driving entrepreneur, would be sitting in to observe it. "Oh no, not her!" she thought. But then she realized that the president's presence there might have been an opportunity in disguise. It was actually an opportunity to get some important concerns out into the open, to demonstrate the kind of good thinking that went on in her team—and much more. The only difference was attitude! A soon as this woman's viewpoint shifted from negative to positive, she could see the goodness in the situation she was facing. That is just one more example of how a good attitude opens our eyes. A bad attitude, in contrast, closes them.

- *We see only the negative things about our fellow voyagers in life and miss the good that is in them.* I am sure you have seen people who have succumbed to the negative pattern of dismissing other people. "I can't rely on Jim," they say. "He's always late." Or "My husband can't be counted upon to get to my son's school events. Everything else takes precedence." This dismissive attitude is very damaging and limiting. Instead of seeing other people's strengths and abilities, our negative outlook causes us to make snap judgments about what they cannot do. We lose their support and help, we lose our ability to become close to other people, and in the end, we diminish the joy of human relationships.

- *We open up a veritable viper's nest of other crippling problems.* We become despondent, pessimistic, and prone to depression. We bring a cynical outlook to all of life's most wonderful events and happenings. We are unable to fully express love. We damage our health. We become much more likely to reach out for the false solace of alcohol and other vices that promise happiness but don't deliver. This list of negatives could go on literally forever because a bad attitude is so terribly damaging to us.

What can we do to chase this negative fellow voyager, this false friend, from our lives? How can we learn to travel in the

company of a more reliable companion—a positive attitude—
that can take our lives to a much higher level of freedom and
happiness?

We can start by admitting that we have a problem with our attitudes.

How good is your attitude? Have the courage to try to answer
that question honestly and openly. Beware of self-justifications
when you answer it because this is an area where they jump in so
quickly. And justifications are a clear indication that a bad attitude has infected your life:

- "I have a good attitude in some areas but a poor attitude
  in others. But I have a right to a poor attitude. I dislike
  my brother because he is a cheater who takes such advantage of me. I am right to feel that way about him."

- "I have a bad attitude because life has dealt me so many
  setbacks. I have a realistic bad attitude."

A good attitude is an absolute, consuming force in life. You
cannot have a positive attitude in 80 percent of your life, or even
95 percent, and allow a negative attitude in the rest. Because that
negative attitude will take over and color everything. Like worry,
it is just that strong a destabilizing force.

If you determine that you have allowed a negative attitude to
gain a foothold in your life, you have taken an important first
step toward chasing it from your life for good. As we have
observed in earlier chapters of this book, admitting that you have
a problem is a first step that must be taken before it can be solved.

Once the problem is out in the open, you are free to make
changes. I believe the suggestions that follow will prove helpful.

We can try to be fully alive in every moment.

In 1939, Thornton Wilder wrote *Our Town* (Perennial, reprint
1998), one of the most beloved plays ever written. It won the

Pulitzer Prize and has never gone out of print—in fact it remains a bestseller even today. In *Our Town*, a young mother named Emily, who has just died, looks down on the earth and asks:

> *Do any human beings ever realize life while they live it— every, every minute?*

And another character answers:

> *No. The saints and poets, they do some.*

Why only saints and poets? Why can't we all be fully alive in each moment, embracing all the wonder and beauty of life? We can. It takes some effort and stretching at first because most of us are accustomed to viewing life in a limited, negative way. But once we taste the joy of living joyfully every day, the floodgates open and we begin a positive new life.

We can test drive a positive attitude for just one day.

Let's assume that you, like many people, are reluctant to make a large commitment to giving your life over to a positive attitude. Who could blame you for being cautious? After all, making such a large change in your outlook is no small thing. People might notice something different about you. Something haywire! Or a positive outlook won't work for you. Perhaps you will try it out and be disappointed when it doesn't produce any changes in your life.

So I would like to ask you to try a modest experiment. For one day only, give yourself over to living with a positive attitude. At the start of just one day, commit yourself to follow these guidelines:

- On that day, you will strive to take that higher road in all activities and encounters.

- You will silently bless others throughout the day.

- You will notice something good about each person you encounter instead of something bad.

- You will give silent thanks to God or a higher power for each good thing that comes into your life.

- You will identify something positive in each situation you encounter.

- You will notice life around you and strive to live in the moment.

- You will draw away from "gripe sessions," negative joke telling, unkind radio commentators, and all other negative influences and orient yourself toward higher activities.

- You will mend some strained human relationships by apologizing, admitting personal wrongdoing, and complimenting others from whom you have felt distanced.

- You will say something kind to strangers or simply smile at them. You will be patient.

After you have given your new attitude a 24-hour test, I guarantee you that you won't want to go back to your old way. If you've been suffering from a negative attitude, your new one will begin to offer you new joys, and new freedoms. With a taste of such joy, a new path will open before you. It is a day that can profoundly change your life.

We can stop worrying about how people will see us in our new, positive role.

Another impediment to living with a good attitude is our fear of projecting a Pollyanna outlook in which we fail to see life's bad events—or naïvely characterize bad events as good. We fear that if we open up the force of positive attitude in our lives, people will see us as old-fashioned, unrealistic, and senselessly optimistic.

There is an antidote to the Pollyanna syndrome. It is simply to have a *realistically* positive attitude. That is not a contradiction in terms. There are so many examples of the power of such an outlook. During World War II, Sir Winston Churchill was magnificently positive and completely realistic at the same time. He didn't miscalculate the tremendous danger Britain faced. He was a complete realist. Yet he was energized and inspired by the challenge, and his outlook kept countless people from becoming decimated by despair. Martin Luther King, Jr., Mother Teresa, Abraham Lincoln, and many other towering figures in world history were all realistic, yet positive thinkers who looked realistically at great problems and decided to attack them with the force of good instead of evil.

Positive realism is not reserved for the great, high and mighty. It is a supremely enabling outlook that is available to us all.

We can resist the lure of criticizing others.

Making negative judgments about other people is something that many people find to be fun. It is surely one of the biggest reasons that people fall into the trap of living with negative attitudes.

Rather than doing our own hard work at growth and progress in our lives, we prefer to point a finger at someone else and say, "That person over there, he's got so many shortcomings! He's not growing. He's not moving ahead with his life. I'm doing a much better job than he is!"

We're true experts at discerning other people's shortcomings. I know that I am very, very good at it. And I have to admit, I often took on just that judgmental role with my late brother, who had health problems through much of his adult life. He was overweight. He had diabetes and heart problems. When I would go to dinner with him, he would often order a steak and french fries. I would look at him and say, "Why are you doing this? Why don't you take better care of yourself? Why don't you change your life?"

I became a terrible nag. And do you know, all my criticism didn't change him at all? Like many people, I believed that it should be easy for other people to change. Yet when I tried to change something about myself, I found that terribly hard.

Over a period of 5 or 6 years, I was keenly aware that I needed to lose 15 pounds. The problem was on my mind morning, afternoon, and night. I didn't like myself because of it. The weight bothered me physically, and it was detrimental to my health. My clothes were too tight. There finally came a day when I realized I had to reserve 5 extra minutes in the morning so I could work the top button of my shirt into place.

I then made a half-hearted attempt to lose weight and discovered that the weight-loss tactics that had worked for me 10 years earlier didn't work any more. My metabolism had changed, which became my excuse for not losing weight. One day when I told my cardiologist this rationalization, he was magnificently uncompassionate. He looked at me and said, "Arthur, eat fewer calories and you will lose the weight." Since then, I've lost 13 of the 15 pounds I need to get rid of.

What am I saying? I am saying that it is very difficult to turn that corner and get going on the changes we must make. Miracles do happen in people's lives, and when they do, the force that's behind them is attitude.

We can develop a hunger for tomorrow.

Saint Paul had a brilliant mind. Through his remarkable letters, we can understand that he overcame many serious problems in his life, but we can also see how his attitude lent him power and strength. Let me paraphrase something Paul wrote in his letter to the Philippians:

> *This one thing I do. I forget what lies in the past and I stretch and strain forward to what lies ahead. I press on toward the goal.*

What was Paul saying? He said, in essence, keep pressing on toward the future.

A number of years ago I was serving in a church in Brooklyn. Across the street from that church was an apartment building, and the superintendent of that building was an ebullient fellow named Ray. He was a Puerto Rican man who was full of aphorisms. He loved to give advice, and he loved to talk.

One day, I found myself in a very down mood. When I ran into Ray, I started complaining and griping about one thing and another.

Ray interrupted me and said, "What's the matter?"

I went right on telling him about things that were going wrong that day.

Ray replied, "I'll tell you something, Reverend. You know what the best thing about today is?"

And I said, "What, Ray?"

And he said, "The best thing about today is that after today comes tomorrow."

I never really thought about that before. After today comes tomorrow! No matter how difficult today seems, tomorrow offers us the chance for a new beginning.

We can keep hope alive.

I believe that we are only beginning to understand the power of hope, which is a central component of a positive attitude. Many of us underestimate hope's tremendous power until we stop to realize that it is the force that has allowed so many of us to survive the most severe tests that life can place before us.

Where have you heard these words, "I never gave up hope"? Those words have been voiced by soldiers who emerged alive from the horrendous battles, by cancer survivors, by mountain climbers who were freezing for days until their rescuers arrived.

Hope, which seems like a tiny little voice in our hearts that we could almost overlook, is really the strongest of forces. Few others are better able to let us survive life's problems by keeping our positive outlook strong. The tiniest thread of hope can provide a bridge from the darkness of any day to a brighter tomorrow.

Deepening Our Understanding

We can choose to go through life with a negative attitude. But if we do, we rob our lives of extraordinary benefits. Armed with positive outlooks, we are better able to:

- *Appreciate the good that other people embody.* Our relationships are enhanced, and we experience the joy of fully connecting with others.

- *Participate in life's most wonderful events and happenings.* Without the burden of negativism, each day becomes more enjoyable and more fully lived.

- *Live freer, more efficient lives.* Negativism ensnares us, weighs us down, and makes even routine activities seem difficult. A positive attitude, in contrast, lifts a weight from our shoulders and brings lightness, ease, and joy to all that we undertake in life.

23
Freedom Follows
Spiritual Searching

I wouldn't be surprised if you had a somewhat suspicious reaction to this chapter's title. If I were in your position, I might too. I would probably be thinking, "Here it comes! Now we'll get the author's pitch for religion! Now he'll start telling us to attend religious services, or, if we do that already, to start going more often! After all, Dr. Arthur Caliandro is a minister."

I want to reassure you that the purpose of this chapter is simply to urge you to begin, or revitalize, your own spiritual search. That search might take you to a church, a mosque, a synagogue, or a mountain. Those are highly personal decisions, and of course they are up to you.

I would like to share my own conviction that making our lives a spiritual adventure, as well as a worldly one, is a step that too many people seem to set aside today. It is a decision that can make all the difference between a life that is simply lived and one that becomes a triumph.

In my last year at Union Theological Seminary in New York, I was taking a course on preaching taught by Dr. Robert McCracken, a great preacher and successor to Harry Emerson Fosdick, himself a legendary preacher. At the end of the year, each student had to deliver a sermon and then have an appointment with Dr. McCracken, who would offer a critique.

It was a difficult process for me. In those days, students were encouraged to arrive at what might be called a *personal theology*—a certain approach to the religious experience that they were expected to express in their trial sermons. Later on, they would take this theology to the churches they served. I was impressed by the sermons given by my fellow students. They were well researched and intellectual in content, and they expressed these theologies in well-structured ways.

I was worried about my sermon. I didn't have a well-organized personal theology that I could articulate. After college and 3 years of seminary, I could only say, in honesty, that Jesus was central to my experience and that I believed in faith. So I stood up and said that and waited for the criticism to follow.

Would Dr. McCracken reprimand me and tell me that I needed to do what my fellow students had done? Would he send me back to the "drawing board" to draft a new statement of theology and then try it out in a second sermon attempt?

He did neither of those things. I was surprised by what he told me:

> *You're fortunate. You're not locked into any system of thinking that, at your stage of life, probably wouldn't be your own anyway. You have the rest of your life to develop your spirituality.*

My life in the years that followed has been influenced by his kindness, and by his words. I have had all of my life to date to engage in a spiritual search that has been ever changing. Over the years, my religious thinking has evolved constantly, taking new forms. I believe that giving up a spiritual search in favor of rigid spiritual beliefs means abandoning something that lies at the very center of spiritual life, which is the openness to new revelations, new ideas, and new experiences.

We need to search, and then search some more, because when we fail to engage in that spiritual journey, we limit our lives in critical ways:

- *We don't take part in the greatest experiment that life offers us.* A spiritual search orients us to the great questions that we face while living: What is our unique purpose in life? What are our gifts? How can we experience life more fully? What is love? How can we deal with life losses and setbacks? After our time on earth, does a realm of new experiences lie before us? These are only a few of the questions that we begin to ask when on a spiritual quest. A spiritual search leads us into a vastly richer and more considered life.

- *We make our experience limited and one dimensional.* Without recognizing the spiritual aspects of everyday experience, we run the risk of dealing only with mundane issues and concerns. At the end of each day, we look back and realize that we thought mostly about driving, running errands, planning meals, and other mundane issues. All of those activities are important, of course. Yet they can become more important if we invest them with an additional, spiritual meaning. For that to happen, we need to try to live life on a deeper level every day.

- *We are blind-sided by life's unexpected events.* Life, as we have noted so many times in this book, holds many surprises for each of us. Often, these surprises test us sorely. Loved ones die. We experience health crises. Our relationships falter or crumble. We lose our jobs. At such times, we are called upon to begin a spiritual search—or more accurately, I might say we are required to "jump start" a spiritual search and get it running at full speed immediately. We suddenly realize that we need some help, some divine assistance, to understand what has happened to us and to recover. Many of us pray for the first time when we are confronted with a crisis. Yet when a spiritual search and practice are already in place, how much better prepared we are to deal with life's troubling events. We have already evolved a context and an understanding of what is happening to us. It is as though we already have a comforting, well-constructed cushion that lets us deal with life's adversities with less destruction in our lives. This cushion can never remove all the pain, or all the learning, from life's big problems. But its presence means we are living a more effective life.

- *We discover that through a spiritual search, we are helped.* This might be the "bottom line." I have seen it happen time and time again. People who thought themselves to be nonbelievers, to be skeptics, to be rugged individualists—call them what you will!—find that their lives are transformed and made freer and better when they embark on a spiritual search. The bottom line is that help comes to us from somewhere when we seek it—not just superficial help but a profound, life-supporting force.

How can we experience these remarkable, life-enriching benefits in our lives?

We can pray.

Not long ago, at a dinner party, I happened to be seated next to a woman I had met about 5 years earlier. I did not know her well, but as we engaged in some small talk, I could sense that something important was on her mind.

"Do you mind if I ask you a question? Are you all right?"

"Yes, why do you ask?"

"I'm sensing a sadness in you. Something inside you is churning and churning."

Almost immediately, two streams of tears came down from her eyes onto her cheeks. She said, "Arthur, I'm going through the most difficult period of my life. I am experiencing unbelievable changes. I am in such pain. I know deep down this will be one of the most important periods of my life. I'm going to achieve enormous growth in it. My head is telling me that, and people are telling me that. But I don't feel it. It just hurts too much. I don't even know how to pray. I can't put a prayer into words."

That gave me a little bit of an opening to offer some spiritual advice. I said, "You're from a Jewish background, aren't you?"

"Yes," she answered.

I said, "I've got a prayer I'd like to give you. I think it will prove helpful to you in your process. Because most of the words in it come from the Psalms, it can fit into any tradition. Would you like it?"

"I would love it," she answered.

I took out a little card and wrote:

Dear God, have mercy on me. Make haste to help me. Rescue me and save me. Do your will in my life.

Then I handed it to her, and I said, "I have found that there is one way that this prayer works best. You've got to say it hundreds and thousands of times so that you're breathing it in and breathing it out, so that it becomes natural to you. When you do this, two things will happen. First, you will begin to feel new reserves of inner strength. Second, remarkable coincidences will start to happen in your life. Things will be brought together in your associations and your relationships. That's the way it works."

I know this woman will benefit greatly from that prayer, which is known in many circles as the Jesus Prayer. Even though that is the name it is known by, it is my belief that it can be adapted and be equally effective whether it is addressed to God, or Allah, or the Great Presence. The fact is, this is a prayer that works in amazing ways.

I believed that the depth of this woman's pain, though disquieting to be sure, could serve as a prelude and an invitation to grow. Even though her heart was not in the struggle that lay before her, she was aware that she was going to grow enormously and that she needed some simple point of spiritual anchoring.

When I began to pray this prayer, I was having a faith crisis. But I decided to give the prayer a try. I recited it almost everywhere I went. It became like a mantra for me, and I suppose I was repeating it thousands of times each day. And after 2 weeks, I have to say that much of my faith crisis disappeared. All manner of coincidences, large and small, began to occur. I was getting answers to the questions that were preying on my mind, and my life became much better.

In my experience, that is how prayer works. To be effective, it must go beyond the intellect. Through it, I have been able to connect with a higher, trusting mind.

In times of such crisis, simplicity is best. It is also best in our daily lives. For this reason, I would urge you to develop a simple practice of prayer, one that can permeate your daily experience. Again, it is best to be flexible and try different approaches. Here are some that have worked for people I have known:

- *A simple, repeated prayer like the one I described just above.* Even the words "Do your will in my life," repeated in your mind through the day, can penetrate into your life, lending a spiritual aspect to all that you do.

- *A period of prayer and reflection each day.* There is no "right" way to pray. I would urge you to simply find a period of every day for quiet reflection. In that time, you might try starting a dialogue where you think and expect your thoughts and questions to be answered. Again, the results of this process might surprise you.

We can stop stretching and straining and find that higher presence within us.

In my early days, I felt a terrible separation from God. He was "up there." I was "down here." How I stretched and strained in my attempts to breach that gap. How I labored whenever I attempted to pray or get in contact with that higher presence.

At some point in my life, my spiritual search led me to a new revelation, that God is within me, in my very center and core. I don't need to project my mind and thoughts out there "somewhere" to touch upon that spiritual presence. I can relax, be calm, and go deep within.

Silence and solitude are of great help in contacting this inner spiritual place. If you find it hard to pray or be in touch with some higher power, I would urge you to simply spend a little time each day quietly, alone. With quiet and calm, you invite a spiritual force into your thinking and into your life.

We can stop beating ourselves up about being "right" or "wrong."

Dr. Norman Vincent Peale, my predecessor at Marble Collegiate Church, made some remarkable progress in helping people define their relationship to faith. One of his greatest contributions is, I believe, overlooked by many people.

At the time Dr. Peale began his ministry, most churches adhered to a theology that was, one might say, harsh and judgmental. Some religious institutions held that people could not encounter God until they became "healed" or until they became so good that God would see their worth and take an interest in them. Other religious institutions became fixated on the notion of sin. To earn God's love, people had to become perfect!

Dr. Peale took a much different approach to these issues. One day, he said to me:

> *Arthur, every single person who comes into this church is broken. We are all broken.*

He was telling me that the religious search is not judgmental or cruel, that everyone was invited to come to our church and was welcome to partake of whatever help he or she found there. I don't know if many people appreciate how unusual this thinking was at the time.

So if you are delaying a spiritual search or not fully engaged in one because you feel you are not worthy or entitled to begin, I would urge you to set that thinking aside. There is a place for everyone at God's table. We are all invited, we can all sit down. Perfection is not the price of admission.

We can bless people.

I mentioned this wonderful idea in Chapter 9, and it also deserves to be highlighted here. There are few more effective ways to invite a spiritual presence into our lives than to go through life silently blessing people.

Bless the cashier in the supermarket. Bless the toll-taker on the highway. Bless the person who is kind to you, bless the person who is unkind. Bless the singer who sings a song that you love. Bless the poet whose words bring new meaning to your life. Bless your house. Bless your children. Bless your job. Bless! Bless! Bless!

You need not be a Christian or a Jew or a Buddhist or a Muslim to do it. Blessing is for everyone. If you spend one day engaged in blessing, you might be amazed at the transformation that takes place in your life.

We can consistently take the higher road.

This is another theme we have touched upon often in this book. Again, it needs to be highlighted in this discussion of spiritual searching. When we are oriented toward it, we realize that most life experiences offer us the choice to take either the higher path, or the lower.

- You can wait a few extra seconds to hold the door for the next user of the cash machine you are leaving—or you can hurry on and let that person deal with it.

- You can allow another driver to enter the road before you, or you can cut her off because you are already running late to work.

- You can talk to your neighbors and get to know them (possibly even share their life experiences and build friendships)—or you can build higher fences and close your doors and mind to them.

- You can tell your children when you feel they have not acted honestly—or you can be silent and avoid a possible conflict.

Choosing the right path in each of life's choices is part of the process of getting your life oriented correctly, in line with all that is best about life. That is another way of describing a spiritual journey.

We can avoid the temptation to seize upon inflexible systems.

How many religions, spiritual systems, and organizations are ready to provide us with ready-made answers we need to life's biggest questions! Our answers can be found by simply believing what they do, following their prescribed steps and rituals. There is little need to think. Theirs is the correct way, and all other ways are wrong. The answers are not to be found by examining our own lives but through the simple quick fix of accepting teachings that are already in place.

In my own early years, I believed what many Christians do: that the only correct spiritual practice was a Christian practice. I had been taught that all other approaches, all other religions, were incorrect. It took me a long time, and much inner reflection, to realize that such thinking is not only wrong but limiting in our quest for spiritual truth.

When rigid beliefs and strictures are allowed to take the place of the hard spiritual work we need in order to grow—when they function as quick fixes—they can only delay, distract, and limit our spiritual growth.

We can love.

Love is the greatest force, the greatest impetus, behind spiritual growth. We can love others. We can love ourselves. We can love our time on earth. We can love the wonder of life, especially its spiritual aspects. We can become agents of love in all we do. We can find an infinite number of ways to let love work in our lives—because love is limitless.

There is no clearer path than love to freedom in our lives. There is no more reliable approach than love to becoming all we were meant to be.

As I close this book and the time we have spent together, let me return to Corinthians, those monumental words that reveal the truth about love and life in images more inspiring than any I could ever pen:

Though I speak with the tongues of men and of angels and have not love, I am become as sounding brass, or a tinkling cymbal. And though I have the gift of prophecy, and understand all mysteries, and all knowledge, and though I have all faith so that I could remove mountains and have not love, I am nothing. And though I bestow all my goods to feed the poor, and though I give my body to be burned, and have not love, it profits me nothing.

Love suffers long and is kind. Love is not envious or boastful. Love is not easily provoked. It does not think evil.

Love doesn't rejoice in iniquity, but in the truth. Love bears all things, believes all things, hopes all things, endures all things.

Love never fails. Prophesies will fail. Tongues will cease. Knowledge will vanish away. For we know in part, and we prophesy in part. But when that which is perfect is come, then that which is in part shall be done away.

When I was a child, I spoke as a child, I understood as a child, I thought as a child. But when I became a man or woman, I put away childish things.

For now we see through a glass, darkly, but then face to face. Now I know in part, but then shall I know even as also I am known.

And now abide faith, hope, charity, these three. But the greatest of these is love.